Confessions of a Mixed-Up Weasel Hater

by

Elizabeth Thomas Wenning

Fame's Eternal Books, LLC
United States of America

Chapter One

"How's the plot, Sam?" Denise asked me. We walked fast to our middle school activities club. I'd see Bobby Bouchard in mine, so I assumed she meant the plan where he falls in love with me.

"I need a miracle," I answered. "He pays *way* too much attention to Amy Cranston. Can we deflate her chest?"

"Can you take Bobby out of your brain for half a sec? I mean the *other* plot, Samantha. Mr. Dubois and Ms. Evans, remember?"

I remembered. Not a lot we could do about them, either. We'd taken Denise's weird dream last summer about a couple of our favorite teachers becoming romantically involved, added a few juicy details, and put it on notebook paper. We thought we'd only committed fiction, though, until we talked to Mr. Dubois.

"We're writers now, Mr. Dubois," Denise announced that autumn afternoon, after school.

"Fantastic!" he responded. I guess all teachers get excited when kids write or read beyond the call of mandatory assignment. "What'd you write about?"

"You and Ms. Evans." Denise said nothing more than those four words. But the *way* she played each syllable out.... I remember wanting to crawl under one of the desks in his classroom.

But Mr. Dubois didn't call us nosy little perverts. Instead, he calmly stroked his beard and said: "I *have* gone out with her."

Denise and I lived on the coincidence for weeks. We vowed to do anything we could to intensify their relationship. But eighth-graders hold little power in such matters. We could only watch and guess— without asking outright—how things progressed. A semester in this limbo had already passed.

"Yes, I remember Mr. Dubois and Ms. Evans," I finally answered Denise. "I don't know what their story is. You know, Mr. Dubois might've made the whole thing up just to play with our trusting little minds."

"Nah, couldn't be." Denise shook her head. "I saw them in the hall together today—*again.*"

"Hear anything mushy?" I tried not to get my hopes up.

"Nah. Maybe next time."

We reached the school library, location of French Club. I said goodbye to Denise and stood outside the door, watching her leave. Denise possessed most of our combined confidence and took it with her when she left. I don't know why it mostly belonged to her. She was kind of plain, really. Skinny, big nose, wore glasses. I was somewhat better looking, but too tall.

Neither of us had much in the boob department. For comfort, I often whispered to myself: "Only middle school. We have time."

I peered through the library door's glass window. Bobby hadn't arrived. Billy Drake had. Geeky, a mere seventh-grader, but pretty harmless. I went in.

At least, I once thought him harmless.

"Hello, Samantha," he said. His voice was a worm's, if worms could talk. And his stance—he stood like a penguin with an upset stomach, or like one of those inflatable clowns that come right back up when you punch them down. Hard to believe he and Denise had liked each other in elementary school. Especially hard to believe for Denise.

"Hi, Drake," I answered. Denise and I called him by his last name—if we talked to him at all. Generally, I tried to be nice to him because of his lingering bad crush on Denise. I knew how unrequited love haunted your whole existence. So to make conversation, I asked him the first question floating into my head. "How do you like Mr. Dubois's class?"

"Oh, fine," Drake said. Can worms sound smug? "I sit there and write nasty things about him all over my desk."

"Well, see you, Drake." So much for kindness. I moved to one of the tables—one far away from Drake's—in the back of the library. How come nobody knew how great Mr. Dubois was except Denise and me? Not just Drake—practically all of Turkey Creek Middle School wallowed in ignorance. But what can you expect from a school that calls its football team the Gobblers?

While I sat contemplating vicious truths to write in the girls' toilet about Billy Drake, Bobby walked in. He said, "Hi." I said, "Hi," back. I didn't even

3

remember to soak up the vision of his gorgeous brown eyes and wavy black hair. If not for Drake's snottiness, I'd have said more to Bobby. Mr. Dubois had helped me for over half a year, listening to my feelings for Bobby and telling me not to be afraid to speak to the boy I thought about constantly. Mr. Dubois said my own shyness was the only reason Bobby didn't fall in love with me. No wonder I liked Mr. Dubois so much. On good days, I even started to believe him. Today, though, I figured him for just another nice adult who didn't know crap.

I watched Bobby stride to his seat. No comparison to a full frontal view, where I could lose myself in those eyes, but . . .

"Are you Samantha Gabreaux?"

I looked up and stared into icy-blue eyes nothing like Bobby's warm brown ones. Below the eyes lay loads of freckles; above them grew lots of curly orange hair. I have no idea why I tried to smile at Frank Stallinger, whom I knew by name only. But to Mr. Dubois's credit, I did smile. "Yes, I'm Sam Gabreaux," I answered.

"I thought so," Frank said, grinning as he stood over my table. If *I* had stood, he'd have been forced to look up at me. Short or not, I'd seen friendlier smiles on Dobermans, and I wondered what he wanted. I didn't wonder long.

"What's the matter with you, anyway?" he demanded, cutting me with his gaze like I was brain-damaged. "How come you're always talking to Mr. Dubois? You madly in love with him?"

"No!" I almost blurted out I loved Bobby Bouchard, but I gained control of myself. More than enough people knew that already, and Frank didn't give me the impression he could be trusted with my business.

"I don't see how you could love him," Frank continued, his attitude like he was emptying a week-old litter box. "Aren't you afraid you'll get AIDS? He's such a *queer*!"

After what Drake had said, Frank's words hit my limit. I stood up and grabbed the back of my chair, wishing I gripped his throat instead. I considered throwing the chair *at* him, then realized I needed it for support—not to mention the damage to my permanent record the first option would have bought me. "Frank!" I started to yell. I wanted to say he sucked, but he might twist it back at me. I thought of calling him a few names, but all of the good insults that sprang to mind could be associated somehow with gay men. Frank could quickly recycle them into more abuse for Mr. Dubois. Finally I settled for "you weasel!" and plopped limply back in my chair. Frank didn't even hear. He just sailed back to his table, looking terribly pleased with himself.

I'd heard people call Mr. Dubois gay before. But the frequency of it had risen lately, and Frank was the first to attack *me* for talking to him. He was also the first to tease me about catching AIDS. I didn't get it. Gay? Denise and I knew Mr. Dubois dated Ms. Evans. But then again, what did we really know, except what Mr. Dubois chose to tell us?

Well, I didn't care. About Mr. D's sexual preference, I mean. The man had practically saved my life last year. See, I'd fought with my ex-friend Tina. She figured out the perfect revenge—telling Bobby I loved him. I'd considered running away to Antarctica. After Bobby knew, he had no excuse not to ask me out—except, of course, that he must not want me, not

5

even a little. Denise and my other friends tried to console me, but it didn't help. Mr. Dubois noticed my misery, and asked me to come see him after school. I did, and he listened to me. Really listened. He let me cry. He didn't tell me to stop loving Bobby, like my parents did when Mom finally badgered the source of my pain from me. Instead he urged me not to be afraid to talk to Bobby, because I was as good as anyone else. Despite Tina's betrayal, I actually talked to Bobby a lot more than before. Me? I couldn't care less who Mr. Dubois spent his spare time with.

But why did so many of the other kids care? Why did they label him gay in the first place? Well, he gave too much homework. Not having his class anymore, maybe I'd grown more tolerant. But that only gave reason not to like him, not reason to make assumptions about his personal life. Okay, so his voice sounded a little higher than some adult males I've heard. And maybe some of his gestures . . . well, *fluttered* a bit. And he wore glasses. And his beard looked weird—only covering the bottom of his chin, like a goat's. Still, no real reason. What did they always say at trials? A man must be assumed innocent until proven guilty. Hey, skinny, wimpy *Frank* wasn't exactly the straightest-looking kid I ever saw. I wanted to tell him so, but I didn't want to stoop to his level.

I also remembered Bobby. Right there in the room. As if I could forget! Had he heard Frank? I glanced over at Bobby's table. For once, seeing him talking to another girl gave me relief. He couldn't have heard. He'd hate me if he knew I was friends with a teacher, let alone one suspected of being gay. Even if Bobby didn't care *personally*, he'd never be able to like me because all the popular kids would make fun of me.

They'd tease him, too, if he loved me. I was clearly doomed.

Ms. Bloch, the librarian who taught us bits and pieces of French for an hour every Friday, arrived. As she drilled us on the phrases we'd learned so far, I occasionally heard Frank laughing with his small group. Once my own name reached my ears, wrapped tightly in unintelligible whispers. Doomed. Even with Frank's pitifully few friends, this would spread through the whole school.

"Samantha, how do you say 'how old are you?' in French?" Ms. Bloch asked.

She had really crammed that one into us, so I automatically knew. I squeaked it: *"Quel age avez-vous?"* A few giggles bubbled through the room. French is quite funny when squeaked. I stole a look at Bobby, who turned away from me, trying to wipe the smile off his face. Definitely doomed.

Unless I stopped my offensive behavior. Maybe if I cut off all contact with Mr. Dubois, this would sputter and die before Bobby got wind of it. I'd miss Mr. Dubois, but sometimes you had to make sacrifices.

And sometimes I could be a real scuzz for even thinking such things. Only a coward would take that option, after all Mr. Dubois had done for me. But maybe I just needed to admit my cowardice and get on with my life. Wasn't a coward not publicly ridiculed better than a brave person splattered with the brown stains of unpopularity?

Finally, after a time like from now back to the dinosaurs, the bell rang. I didn't bolt, but I slipped quickly into the hall. I headed for the auditorium, the site of Denise's activity. Denise leaped out looking bright and happy, like practically always. Drama with her would have been fun, acting out plays and stuff—

but by the end of the semester I'd have had to act in front of other people. No way. Besides, Bobby had chosen French. We shared a common interest in the language. We both came from French and Native American ancestors. I liked exploring my heritage. Besides, one extra hour a week with Bobby was one extra hour a week. Billy and Frank didn't add ambiance, however. God only knew why they took French.

"How was French?" Denise asked, when she sighted me.

"Disgusting."

"Bobby didn't notice you today? You poor, poor baby." She used the same tone on her family's cats.

"Oh, he noticed me, I guess. He noticed me screw up in French class because some . . . *weasel* upset me."

"You mean *you* noticed someone in French Club besides Bobby? There *is* a God!" exclaimed Denise. "Who?"

"Fr . . . ." I stopped before finishing the name. How much could I tell Denise without her thinking me scum for avoiding Mr. Dubois? *If* I decided to do that. "Oh, just some dumb seventh-grader. You don't know him." I lied. Denise did know Frank, at least by name. As much as I had, before today.

"Well, what did he do?" she asked, as we walked down the hall towards the big front doors. Or towards the turn leading to Mr. Dubois's room.

"What did he do?" I tried stalling. Hmm. If I only told her Frank accused me of loving Mr. Dubois, Denise would probably understand if I didn't want to see our favorite teacher for a while. She'd think I was just trying to prove Frank lied, which he did. But if I mentioned Frank crying "queer," then she'd know I'd given in to other people's prejudices. Which would not be cool with Denise.

"Oh," she interrupted, as we reached the turn. "Do you want to visit Mr. Dubois before we leave?"

"No! Uh, I mean, not today. Let's just go home. I'll tell you more when we get outside and away from people."

"Okay."

A few more steps and we crossed into the cold. Not freezing—Michigan January thaw, and slushy, but a lot better than less-than-zero wind chill. Herds of kids thinned out along the sidewalks, and finally I could talk quietly to Denise without too much fear.

"Anyway, this kid said I was in love with Mr. Dubois."

"Did Bobby hear?" After her previous sarcasm, her understanding surprised me.

"I don't think so." I didn't say anything else, and I hoped she'd leave it alone. She did. But I kept thinking as we trudged down the sidewalks, past numerous bare trees. Turkey Creek Middle School was a brutal place to attempt survival. People didn't often beat each other up. Nobody brought in guns—yet. But these kids could still wreck your life beyond repair. Especially if you still possessed emotions, especially if your popularity did not radiate from you like nuclear energy gone severely wrong. Me, I was fair game for anyone who *did* glow popular. Or anyone who wanted to, like Frank. I'd survived so far, but only because I never brought any attention to myself. I blended into the background—chameleons wore stripes with plaids compared to me. Frank might drag me into the open unless I gave him no more rope.

One strange thought rushed into another. By the time Denise left me at my doorstep, I'd imagined

Frank dressed in a white sheet and burning a cross on my lawn for "associating with queers." I managed to say goodbye to Denise, and hello to my mom when I came in the house. My dad wasn't home from work yet, and thank God, I had no brothers or sisters. If I'd had a stupid brother—say, about a year younger than me—he'd go to Turkey Creek too, and know about Mr. Dubois. Then I'd have no safe place whatsoever.

I pushed straight into my bedroom and closed the door. I flipped on my stereo and examined my bookshelves. My gaze landed on a three-volumed boxed set from Christmas, still unopened. J.R.R. Tolkien's *The Lord of the Rings*. I hadn't seen the movies yet. Neither my parents nor Denise were interested in that sort of thing—this was a gift from a friend of the family. I'd liked Harry Potter well enough, though—and movies didn't last long enough for what I needed now, anyway. I tore off the plastic and pulled out the first book, *The Fellowship of the Ring*. I lay down on my bed, and proceeded to lose myself in it. Absolute change from reality: people only three feet tall, elves taller than me, and wizards. While I read, I didn't need to decide whether or not I'd avoid Mr. Dubois. I even lost concern enough to be amused that one of the characters was named Sam, too. We even had the same last initial, if not the same sex. So I spent the weekend, flicking worries away as I turned pages.

Chapter Two

Unfortunately, I woke up the following Monday. I tunneled under the covers. My mom had to yell at me five times before I finally resurfaced. I figured I'd better not give her any more reason for suspicion. I wanted to stay home, but I knew that without a temperature of 103, Mom would demand to know the cause. She'd manage to drag the whole story out of me. Mom had the best heart, but she could squeeze operational secrets out of the most determined Al Qaeda terrorist. The C.I.A. should draft her.

Not ready to tell her about French Club and Frank, I got dressed and ate my cereal as usual. Mom wouldn't understand. She was like Denise—brave. She'd think me stupid. I knew, because whenever she spent an hour or so forcing me to confess whatever worried me at the time, she'd end up calling me silly to brood over something so trivial. Maybe she'd be right again, but I still hated her labeling all my problems idiotic.

I made the mistake of hugging her a little tighter before I cleared the front door, though.

"Something the matter, honey?" she asked. Maybe she knew me better than other mothers knew their kids because she only had me. No other kids to divide her attention.

"No, Mom," I lied. I dashed down the porch steps and onto the street before she interrogated further. I started for my friend Maria's house. See, I walked home with Denise, but I walked to school with Maria. I couldn't wait for Denise to come pick me up—I had to get to Turkey Creek early. More time to look at Bobby that way. Not that he got there early most days, but the anticipation wouldn't let me wait for Denise. So I always went to Maria's, hurried her out of her house, and on to the only guaranteed accessible Bobby-watching grounds in town.

I'd lost all urge to hurry this morning, but Maria expected me. Even though I'd thought all weekend about the Dubois question, I still hadn't made a decision. I leaned, though—leaned towards keeping my distance from him for a while. Nothing permanent. When Frank had been thrown off my scent and had busied himself tormenting someone else, I'd talk to Mr. Dubois again.

As much as Frank and the popular people scared me, I knew things could be worse. I could have been a boy. Then I'd really catch it for talking to Mr. Dubois. But things were bad enough with female plumbing. The talk of AIDS. Never mind that to actually infect me, Mr. Dubois would probably have to engage in extremely heterosexual—let alone abusive and illegal—behavior. People at Turkey Creek didn't think all that logically. Even aside from AIDS, my sex didn't matter—at least not enough. The way most kids saw it, if you hung around more than absolutely necessary with someone suspected of a certain perversion, then you must share that perversion. Or some other shocking deviation. Our town wasn't big enough for any of us to have known from elementary school onward that someone in our class had two mommies, or two daddies. And apparently the *Oprah* show hadn't sunk in with all that many people.

If the Dubois situation didn't trouble me enough, I could always worry about starting my stint as a kindergarten aide that day. I wasn't sure I could stand little kids. I knew I couldn't stand home science or industrial arts, my other choices. But what if the kids morphed into total brats whenever the teacher left the room?

Despite all the stuff knocking around in my head, I reached my first stop without a truck squishing me. I rapped on the door of the small brick house where Maria Juarez-Smith lived with her mother and sister. Something about Maria always cheered me up. She was . . . well, innocent. I'm not saying she didn't know about sex. That's not it at all. You could just see Maria would never be cruel to anyone or any*thing*. I saw it in the way she took such good care of her hamsters and parakeets. Her animals liked and trusted her, and animals know good people. A reasonably smart dog probably wouldn't eat prime steak from Frank Stallinger's hand.

Maria answered the door, blue-and-white parakeet perched on her left shoulder. Her round face and brown eyes looked sleepy, she still had her road-killed fuzzy purple bath robe on, and her straight brown hair hung tangled. But she smiled at me, even though she probably believed I'd yell at her for running late. I didn't. I sat in her family's kitchen, mindlessly sipping a glass of water while she showered and dressed. Maria's older sister, Roxanna, had already left for Audubon High, and their mother had already gone to work. She worked at the post office with my dad, and when Maria's parents were still married, her dad had worked there, too. When we were little, our families used to visit, and we'd play together. So I'd known Maria for ages. That's why I still talked to her, even though she was only a seventh-grader. Besides, I wasn't popular enough to afford turning my nose up at younger friends.

By the time she came downstairs, I definitely wanted to talk to her—sorta. "Maria," I asked her, "if you had a habit—not a very popular habit, but *you* liked it—but you knew someone you loved wouldn't approve, what would you do?"

"What?"

I repeated my question. She looked at me for a moment, then said: "Well, I guess I'd give up the habit, Sam." Maria knew I talked to Mr. Dubois, and she once told me she found it pretty weird. She excused me because I had no siblings and didn't know any better, having been surrounded by adults all my life. She never said anything bad about Mr. Dubois himself—never said anything about it anymore. She probably thought my "habit" involved reading tabloids to maple trees, or something.

When we reached Turkey Creek, I left Maria with one of her seventh-grade friends and traveled to the front of the building to look for Denise—and Bobby. Neither had arrived yet, but Billy Drake already polluted the morning with his presence. He stood— with his unmistakable stance—by the north doors, and he babbled at another seventh-grader, a girl.

"Dubois is so gay!" giggled Drake.

"Extremely homosexual," the girl agreed. "I told my dad, and he says they should clean the schools of people like him."

"Same at my house," Drake replied.

14

My guts lurched. That settled it. Denise arrived soon after, then the bell rang. The only thing to quiet my stomach as we stepped over the threshold into Turkey Creek was knowing I wouldn't be visiting Mr. Dubois for a while.

The worst part of helping in the kindergarten room second hour turned out to be that the only way to get there led directly past Mr. Dubois's room. He always stood out in the hallway between hours to make sure nobody fought. Somehow I managed to slip past him that first Monday, and I actually enjoyed the class. Another girl, Bethany Williams, worked the second hour shift with me, and we got along okay. She played the classroom piano when Ms. Pole, the kindergarten teacher, let her. I love watching people play instruments, even though Bethany mostly learned hymns. But surprisingly, the kids gave the most satisfaction. Some of them did have bratty tendencies, but I had even more at their age, so tolerance came easily enough. None of them spread rumors about anyone being gay, at least. Five-year-olds held certain advantages over my peer group.

I especially liked Janna, a little girl with gorgeous dark eyes who looked like she could have been Bobby's baby sister. A tomboy, but brattiness-free. I told her stories, some I made up, and some out of old books from my own childhood. She seemed to like the stories, and she helped me when I straightened up the classroom.

Tuesday proved identical to Monday except for a conversation with Denise in the lunch line.

"I talked to Mr. Dubois a little while ago," she said, digging her money out of her pocket as we neared the head of the line.

"Yeah?" I forgot I wasn't supposed to care.

"Yeah. He thinks you're mad at him. He says you walked right by him in the hallway the past two days and didn't even say 'hi.' *Are* you mad at him?" she asked.

So he *had* seen me. And Denise had forgotten what Frank said, about me loving Mr. Dubois, or she wouldn't ask the question. Unless she thought I blamed Mr. Dubois for something not his fault. "Of course not," I told her. "Why should I be? Next time you see him, tell him I'm not mad, okay?"

"Why don't you?" Denise gave me one of her suspicious looks.

I stared at the ceiling, took a deep breath, and let it out slowly. "Denise, I didn't want to tell you, because you won't like it. Remember what happened in French Club last week? I'm staying away from Mr. Dubois for a while, just until people stop calling me abnormal for talking to him without being forced. I'd die if Bobby heard about it."

Denise looked at me, unable to completely hide her contempt. How would she look if she knew I avoided Mr. Dubois because of the gay rumors, too? At any rate, she didn't say anything more on the subject.

A week later, I fell apart.

The kindergarten kids had gym that day, and Ms. Pole went with them. This meant Bethany and I had a half-hour to goof off before they came back. I wanted to arrive before Bethany, though, so I could practice some stuff Denise taught me on the piano without an audience. Denise could play even better than Bethany, because her parents sent her to lessons for *everything*. Where she found time to hang out with me at all, I have no idea.

16

Even though beating Bethany meant giving up my last few glances at Bobby as we left social studies, I ran out of first hour and dashed down the hall to the kindergarten room.

"Hello, Samantha," said Mr. Dubois. He threw his arms wide in one of his fancy gestures before I could possibly dodge him. What could I do? I looked everywhere, wondering if anyone heard my heart pounding, besides me. I didn't spot Bobby, or any of his friends. Frank did not crouch in the shadows near the drinking fountain waiting to scream, "Samantha Gabreaux's at it again!" I tossed Mr. Dubois a hasty "hi," turned around, and flew for the door of the kindergarten room.

I slammed the door shut behind me. Thank God I beat Bethany. After checking the glass in the top of the door for cracks, I automatically began my new morning ritual, opening the teacher closet and looking in Ms. Pole's gilded mirror. I wanted to see what I had looked like for first hour with Bobby. Stupid, futile idea. If I did look bad, nothing could help me by *then*. But I still needed to know.

My reflection, even after I pushed a stray piece of my thick brown hair back into place, scared me. My gray-green eyes wore a terrible hunted look, like those of a rabbit about to be shredded by a wolf. Had Mr. Dubois seen the same fear-crazed mammal?

I shut the closet door and sank into the teacher's chair. What had I done? Why did I let myself do it? After the countless ways Mr. Dubois had helped me! Some of the small gestures came rushing back. The time he had tried so hard to make me laugh after I found out Bobby was taking Lori Fowler to the Halloween Dance. The time he had sung that stupid song—"You Are My Sunshine"—to me when he learned I'd missed Bobby's solo in the Eighth Grade Chorus's Christmas program. And, of course, the whole mess with Tina before she and I made up, then drifted apart without malice. Only scum could act like I had after all his kindnesses. I was no better than Frank Stallinger or Billy Drake—and maybe worse. *They* owed Mr. Dubois no loyalty. Pain started in my throat and grew harder and harder, so bad I didn't even worry how I'd explain crying if Bethany came in.

Tears slid down my cheeks and my nose, and I grabbed some of Ms. Pole's tissues to wipe them away. I just kept wiping. I wished I could wipe away the last several days.

Maybe I could. Well, not exactly. I couldn't erase the videotape, so to speak, but I could shoot new footage. I could apologize to Mr. Dubois and never act so stupid again. The pain in my throat eased. By the time Bethany got there, I hopped up on one of those midget kindergarten tables and told her to bang out "Amazing Grace."

When the bell beeped the end of second hour, I ran straight to Mr. Dubois.

"Hi!" I smiled, wide as I could. "Mr. Dubois, can I talk to you after sixth hour? It's kind of important."

"Yeah, sure, Sam. Good to see you." I hadn't spoken to him for at least a week, and he was ready to spare me some time after school, like nothing significant had passed.

Later, Denise came with me to Mr. Dubois's room. I apologized for ignoring him and told him how it had started, but I didn't repeat everything Frank said. I didn't want to hurt him with the stupid rumor. Mr. Dubois, great soul, didn't fuss over what I had done, or not done. He just said, "I'm glad you're talking to me again, Sam." Like he actually missed me instead of

18

enjoying the time without me around, moaning over Bobby!

Mr. Dubois didn't hear all of Frank's disgusting remarks, but Denise dragged them out of me on the way home. I also admitted that she did know who'd called Mr. Dubois gay, and identified Frank.

"He should talk!" Denise sputtered. I laughed, because Frank didn't mirror my vision of masculinity, either. Why should he put down Mr. Dubois?

Through the whole mess, I'd read *The Lord of the Rings* faithfully. I'd now drunk deeply of the second book, *The Two Towers*, and that night after I got home I absorbed the part where Sam Gamgee fought the giant spider Shelob to save his friend Frodo. Made me glad I'd talked to Mr. Dubois. Couldn't have one Sam acting courageous and loyal, and the other one the exact opposite.

Yet, in the books at least, Sam Gamgee had no love interest. He had probably never heard of middle school. He could afford courage.

Chapter Three

A couple weeks after I started visiting Mr. Dubois again, the weather turned freakishly warm. Everybody loved it, but Mr. Dubois was manic. Convinced it would hold through the weekend and he could lower his sailboat into the lake, he proposed an outing for the Sailing Club. I'd been in Sailing Club last semester, before French. Due to one complication after another, we hadn't actually *sailed* the previous term.

"If it looks like it'll freeze up again," he assured me, "I can always hoist it back up for a while." I couldn't argue with him. Nobody could. He invited me along, even though I no longer belonged to Sailing Club. He said Denise could come too, even though she'd never been in it at all.

Denise responded enthusiastically when I relayed the invitation, until she remembered.

"*This* Saturday afternoon? Piano lesson. Mom gets spastic when I even *think* about missing one." Apparently, Denise's mom had been pretty close to famous for her piano playing before she got married. Maybe that's why she obsessed over Denise's lessons. Well, even without Denise, I still wanted to go sailing with Mr. Dubois. And since he'd set it for Saturday, no one would know about it except other kids who went. Kids who'd be highly unlikely to criticize me to Frank—or Bobby—for the same thing they themselves did. So all I had to do was convince my parents that Mr. Dubois wasn't completely insane for wanting to take a bunch of kids sailing in early February.

"The man's got to be an idiot," said my father, from the depths of his recliner.

"No, he's not," said my mother, moving in front of the television so that her hips totally blocked my father's view of the local news. "If Mr. Dubois says it'll be all right, I'm sure it will be. He really cares about Samantha, and I'm sure it'll be good for her to get out with other kids. Denise is hardly ever available for her on the weekends."

Last time we had parent-teacher conferences, Mom talked to Mr. Dubois even though I didn't have his class anymore. They talked about *me* the whole time. They made me sit far enough across the room from them that I couldn't hear. But anybody can lip-read well enough to recognize her own name—mentioned by both, several times. After missing some spectacular footage of flames consuming a three-story house in Detroit, my father gave his permission, and my mother stopped obstructing his view.

On Saturday, the weather still held. My mother waited in the car while I knocked on Mr. Dubois's door. When he appeared, she waved and backed out of the driveway. Mr. Dubois ushered me in. I had never seen his house before. Nice enough, but extremely simple. I could only see one television—small, black-and-white. His stereo looked no better than the one in my bedroom. I didn't find a microwave in the kitchen. An unmarried man who could survive without a microwave. Impressive, but Frank would probably consider it further evidence of homosexuality. My counter-evidence, however, sat on the love seat in the living room, fairly attractive for a woman in her early thirties. A little weird to see her in jeans and tennis shoes, though.

"I thought Ms. Evans could go with us, as a chaperone for the girls," Mr. Dubois explained.

"Great!" I said. Not only did her mere presence count as proof something really existed between these two—he could have asked any female teacher, right?—but I would spend the afternoon observing their interaction. I couldn't wait to report back to Denise.

"And now I'm glad I did," Mr. Dubois continued. "You were the only sure bet to show up, Sam. A few maybes, but now it doesn't look like they're coming. The entire school board would have spontaneously combusted if I took one girl out sailing by myself."

Well, my troubles would grow, but Mr. Dubois's image with the kids could only be improved by such an incident. I didn't know if my solo appearance absolutely proved Mr. Dubois's unpopularity, or if I had the only parents derelict enough to let their kid go sailing in February. Probably some of each. Jeez, I was the only one! Mr. Dubois's biggest fan. I'd really be ruined if Frank ever found out. Or Bobby. But how would they? Who was here to blab?

Then I thought about Mr. Dubois and Ms. Evans. If not for me, they could sail by themselves and enjoy each other a lot more. But I could do nothing now. My mother had long gone. She'd headed for the mall without her cell phone, too. Stuck, so I might as well have fun. I loved the water, and I loved the weather, no matter how abnormal for Michigan this time of year. Warm was warm. And maybe one kid was easier to forget than several. Maybe Mr. Dubois and Ms. Evans would let down their guard in front of me.

Mr. Dubois led us out to his backyard, which lay on the green canal leading to the Clinton River. The Clinton in turn flowed to Lake St. Clair. On the canal floated the reason his house had so much empty space. Not only did Mr. Dubois possess an exquisite twenty-four-foot sailboat, but he also owned the set-up that had allowed him, all winter, to hold it hoisted high above the recently frozen water line. The huge tarp that protected the boat from the effects of snow and wind sprawled in the garage we'd passed through on our way out. Not for Mr. Dubois the inconvenience of storing his most precious treasure at a marina. He couldn't have taken as easy advantage of this freak thaw if he'd done that.

Apparently Mr. Dubois—and maybe Ms. Evans, maybe a stronger neighbor—had lowered the sailboat into the canal before I arrived. So nothing remained but to board it, strap those hideous orange life jackets on, and motor out to the lake. Once on the St. Clair, Mr. Dubois cut the outboard.

"Okay, Sam," he said, "do you remember all your knots and cleating from last semester?"

"Uh-huh." I did, vaguely. And so far, no seasickness rose within. I'd have died before showing myself to Mr. Dubois as one of those inferior people who heave the second they leave land. Anyway, Ms. Evans and I helped him put up the mainsail and the jib, and soon we glided across the lake.

Unfortunately, Mr. Dubois and Ms. Evans did not forget my presence, though I tried to be quiet. They didn't kiss, they didn't whisper to each other, they didn't even touch each other. The pair did nothing concrete I could throw at Frank, or Billy Drake, or anybody else if they started calling Mr. Dubois gay again. Not that I had the guts to say anything anyway, but it would have been nice to *have* the proof, even if I never used it. Yet I saw *something*. I mean, for me personally, after that day no doubt remained. Those two were in love. They looked at each other a lot, like I looked at Bobby—only they looked at *each other*. And an extra gentleness stole into Mr. Dubois's voice, even when he supposedly talked to me.

"This is so beautiful," I said. We had traveled a fair distance from shore, and Mr. Dubois let me hold the tiller and steer for a while. The deep blue of the water, the little whitecaps of the waves, the sound of the wind catching the sails, the clean smell—*beautiful* was the only word to surface from my vocabulary. Well, *chilly* surfaced too—I *was* a little colder out on the water than back at the house. I appreciated the sweater my mother made me bring, though I'd never admit it to her. But sensory joy came cheap at the price of an occasional shiver.

"Yes, it's gorgeous," agreed Mr. Dubois, looking at Ms. Evans. "But it gets better. Do you know, Sam, you can sail from here up the St. Clair River into Lake Huron, under the Mackinac Bridge and into Lake Michigan, and all the way to Chicago?"

"Wow." I hoped he understood my quietness as sincerity.

"I did that last summer, with some friends. I might do it again this year." Mr. Dubois looked at Ms. Evans. He did not invite her to accompany him in front of me. I'd have willingly bet my allowance for the rest of the year, however, that when summer came the two of them would shove off together, alone, on exactly that route. Unless they had a big fight between now and then, or one of them got squished by a truck.

"Stopped for a while on Mackinac Island," Mr. Dubois continued. "You ever been there, Sam?"

"No, but it sounds neat." My parents never took me anywhere. They didn't leave me with relatives while they traveled to exotic destinations—*they* never went anywhere, either. My grandparents took me as far as a cottage in the northern part of the Lower Peninsula when I was six, but that formed the extent of my travels. Just sailing around on Lake St. Clair meant adventure to me. But I wanted to go to Mackinac Island one day. A place with no cars, just horses and bicycles, appealed to me.

Gradually, the lake began to grow rougher. *I will not throw up,* I chanted in my head as the boat leaned heavily to one side. But I'm sure I looked green, though somehow Mr. Dubois did not notice. Ms. Evans turned green enough for both of us. Mr. Dubois noticed *her* immediately and decided to sail for home.

My mother hadn't shown up by the time we tied up the boat. Mr. Dubois brought us in the house, and got us all pop. He put a CD on his stereo. Some kind of rain forest music—each adult has at least one flaw. I started on my second pop and had helped make a dent in a large bowl of chips when my mother honked from the driveway. I said my goodbyes and scurried out to her.

"Am I late?" my mother asked, when I opened the car door and sat down. "Did the other parents pick up their kids already?"

"Yeah, but you're not *real* late. No big deal," I told her. Letting her believe I had spent quality time with members of my peer group would not hurt her. We would both be happier this way.

The weather snapped cold again by Valentine's Day. Not freezing, so Mr. Dubois technically didn't have to hoist the boat, but cold. Valentine's Day fell on a Wednesday, and I went happily to my first hour social studies class, the one with Bobby. Despite the incident with Frank, I'd managed to talk to Bobby more, as Mr. Dubois advised. By now Bobby considered me a friend—even if my lack of popularity made me one he didn't want to display prominently. And I considered him a friend too, aside from desperately wanting him to love me. I actually enjoyed talking to Bobby. We had similar family backgrounds, except he had sisters and I had nothing but parents. We'd compare our cousins, our aunts and uncles, and the crazy stuff our dads complained about. He'd tell me what his father said on some issue, like how the liberals funneled all the money from decent taxpayers straight to special interest groups, and I'd have to admit *my* father had said the same thing two nights before. I found it comforting. Denise's parents contrasted with mine like Frank Stallinger's looks contrasted with Bobby's. They voted for the people my and Bobby's fathers griped about. I think Denise's parents even lived in a commune once. I mean, we're talking *different* here. And Denise was different too, like her parents. Don't get me wrong. Denise, my best friend, understood the important parts of life. And her parents treated me great—I liked them. But Bobby's home environment sounded more familiar. I could discuss a surprising number of things more comfortably with Bobby than with Denise.

And, of course, there was what he and I called "the French-Indian thing." I've never suffered from being one-sixteenth Native American—Sioux and Ojibwa. You can't even see it in me, though in the summertime my father and my uncle tan a deep, reddish brown. I doubt I'll benefit from it, either, because one-sixteenth is a far cry from the one-quarter that gets you a full academic scholarship to college. Aside from the scholarship thing, which would be nice, I'd never want to claim any kind of minority status I didn't really earn. Neither would Bobby, I don't think. But he was one-eighth Ojibwa, and even had some known, distant cousins on the reservation up by Mount Pleasant. Yet, fractional as our heritage was, it affected us. Bobby thought of it primarily as Native American, but I think the combination of French and Indian culture had become a separate thing, differing from either of the parts that made it. At any rate, though Bobby was proud to be French-Indian, he didn't want to talk about the hunting and trapping each of our fathers did after work during the winter with anyone but me, and vice-versa. In addition to Denise and her cats, and Maria and all of her pets, a large segment of the ruling crowd at Turkey Creek were well on their way to joining PETA. Funny—we were all fair enough game for cruelty to *each other*. Bobby's good looks, purely average academic effort, and general coolness had bought his membership into the Turkey Creek elite, but apparently he did not think these qualities enough to make up for a dad who harvested muskrats. As for me, I had enough problems with the Dubois thing without advertising my father's politically incorrect hobbies. How did *I* feel? I loved Denise, and Maria. I loved *pet* animals, in any case. But I also loved my dad, loved Bobby, and couldn't truly condemn anything that bound us together.

Bobby and I also liked some of the same television shows—not nearly cultural enough for Denise's parents to allow into their living room. One show had been moved this season to the same time as my absolute favorite, so I watched my favorite show every Tuesday night, and Bobby filled me in on the other program Wednesday morning. We had a DVD player, but this was more fun. Since Mrs. Higuerra had me sitting behind Bobby, it provided an excellent excuse for him to turn around and let me drink in those gorgeous brown eyes.

So I liked Valentine's Day falling on a Wednesday. I didn't have a card for Bobby. I didn't want to give valentines to anyone else, so to show up with one just for him would be too conspicuous. Tina had already told him how I felt last year. I didn't want to give him a pathetic reminder when I knew he would not have a card for me. But maybe I'd just say it—wish him a Happy Valentine's Day, like he'd think I'd do for anyone—and then he could say it back, just to be polite.

Maybe later. First things first.

"What happened on *The Mannings* last night, Bobby?"

He turned to face me, dark eyes wide. "Oh, Sam. You should've seen it. Jim got killed at the end. Wendy shot him. Blood sprayed all over the place."

"He's really dead?" I asked. "You're sure they won't somehow get his heart started?"

"No, he's dead, Sam. I watched the preview for next week. They were burying him. Black clothes and umbrellas."

"But I didn't want him to die!" I didn't tell Bobby, but Jim kind of reminded me of him, grown up.

"Well, he managed to shoot Wendy back before he died," Bobby said. His face fell in sympathy with my grief. "Her funeral made the preview, too."

I did feel better. Not because Wendy died, but because Bobby cared enough to try consoling me. But he turned back around in his seat and began examining his social studies assignment before I could say "Happy Valentine's Day." I let myself stare at the back of his head for a while. I'd almost returned to my own assignment when the reappearance of those magnificent eyes blessed me.

I know I go on forever about Bobby's brown eyes, but they differed from anyone else's. Sometimes they held warmth, even understanding, like when he saw Jim's death had upset me. Sometimes they contained mystery, and I'd be hypnotized by one of his gazes looking right through me like I didn't exist. A couple times I've seen anger in Bobby's eyes—so strong I could only weakly thank God I hadn't caused it. But this time Bobby's eyes overflowed with mischievous glee. I wondered what could possibly spark such a glow. "Sam! I almost forgot to tell you! My cousin Joe took me out to eat last night before *The Mannings*."

Bobby's cousin Joe was twenty-two years old and drove a truck for a living. I knew the attention of his older cousin flattered Bobby, but that alone could not bring such sheer amusement to his eyes. I stared at my love. I felt my eyebrows crinkle—I probably looked pretty stupid.

"You'll never guess who we saw eating out together last night!" Bobby continued, smiling so wide at me my heartbeats all blurred together. "Guess, I dare you."

I opened my mouth to say I had no idea, but before I could form the words, Bobby leaned closer to me. He blurted out: "Mr. Dubois and Ms. Evans!"

Even knowing what I knew, his news amazed me. "No! You're kidding!" I responded. Bobby knew, now, too. I reached oneness with him then, even more intensely than when we talked about our families. He had discovered something incredible and shared it with *me*! Not only that, but his face hovered so close to mine that if I moved an inch, our lips would touch. . . .

"I'm not kidding," Bobby said to me before I had much time to hold that thought. "I even . . . ." He trailed off, lowering his voice, and asked: "Are you ready for this?"

I nodded excitedly.

"I even saw him kiss her," he whispered.

I barely stopped myself from screaming, "YES!!!" loud enough to break the windows. Hopefully, Bobby only told me about his sighting because he thought it bizarre and newsworthy, not because he knew I was friends with Mr. Dubois. I didn't want to give myself away now. I had yet another problem. At the risk of seeming crude, I *had* to ask.

"Did they . . . well, do you think they Frenched?"

"As far as I could tell, Sam. I tried not to stare," Bobby said. "I guess you can't believe everything you hear," he added.

He'd never been more right. I sang inside. Oh, yeah, I already knew what I knew. But what was I supposed to say to Frank? That I'd seen Mr. Dubois and Ms. Evans *looking* at each other? This, on the other hand rose definite, stood concrete. Beautiful proof, amazing, fabulous proof. Frank and Billy and all the rest were *wrong*, and I could rub it in their faces some day when I attained bravery.

But what if Bobby lied? I mean, all I had was his word. But why would Bobby lie? Why lie like *this*? If Bobby wanted to lie, he would've lied against Mr.

Dubois, not for him. Denise told me once that last semester she'd heard Bobby saying the same things Frank and Billy did about Mr. Dubois. I got mad at Bobby for two whole days after that—a record. Well, not *much* of a record, because it spanned a weekend and Bobby never noticed, but a record. Bobby had completely made up for his error now, though. He had turned again, but I tapped him gently on the shoulder. "Happy Valentine's Day, Bobby," I whispered, smiling.

"The same to you, Sam."

After class I ran to catch Denise coming out of her first hour. I quickly relayed everything I'd learned from Bobby, including the part about tongues.

"Great!" she shrieked. "This is *way* better than what you told me about sailing. Our plot is definitely for real! I'm psychic," she continued more quietly, in awe of herself. "I dreamed it all."

I felt awe for someone else. "And you said Bobby only made good eye candy!"

"Well, he *was* the last person I expected to come up with such spectacular information."

"Not the *last* person," I sniffed.

"Yeah, you're right," she admitted.

"You bet I'm right. This proves Bobby is a much better person than Frank Stallinger—in case you doubted. If Frank saw Mr. Dubois kissing Ms. Evans, would he tell me about it?"

"No," replied Denise, in full retreat. Maybe I'd attacked a little roughly, but the fact she never *really* approved of my pursuit of Bobby hurt me, even though she remained sympathetic and loyal. "I just wish Frank *had* seen it," she finished.

"Oh well, I'm just as glad it was Bobby. Do you know he wished me Happy Valentine's Day?" Only a slight exaggeration. I might have punctuated the question with my best imitation ballet leap across the hallway, but I had enough image problems.

"Besides," I continued, giddily, "maybe the next time one of those weasels says something offensive, I'll throw them Bobby's evidence. They'll probably drop dead of shock." I smiled wider, picturing the black clothes and umbrellas. Though I still kept hearing kids every day chattering about Mr. Dubois's alleged gayness, nobody had said anything to me personally since Frank. Maybe someday I actually would find the courage to tell them all off.

"I doubt it, Sam," said Denise, interrupting my visions of hope and glory. "And we shouldn't tell the weasels about it, either." She had grown thoughtful. "It's their tough luck if they're stupid enough to care whether Mr. Dubois is gay. They're not worth the effort it would take to tell them. Besides, do you think they'd believe you? People like Frank and Billy just believe what they want." Denise's voice rose steadily. "Wouldn't have done any good if Frank *had* seen it instead of Bobby!" she declared. "And Billy Drake! If he'd seen Mr. Dubois at the restaurant with Ms. Evans, *he'd* try telling everyone Mr. Dubois was *bisexual*!"

My bubble burst. Denise made several good points. And maybe Mr. Dubois wouldn't *want* us telling all sorts of people he dated Ms. Evans. I mean, he told Denise and me like it was no big deal. But maybe it was only no big deal because he liked us and trusted us to keep our mouths shut. Even if Mr. Dubois didn't care, I could now clearly imagine telling Frank. Frank would reply: "Yeah, you're just making it up because you *love* the queer." I'd say he could ask Bobby Bouchard, because he'd seen it. Bobby'd just love having a dweeb like Frank asking him questions. And if Bobby stooped to answer, maybe Frank would start hounding *him*, saying Bobby only covered up for his own gay affair with Mr. Dubois. No one at Turkey Creek would believe that about Bobby, but even so— so much for courage.

Denise and I had been walking towards our lockers while having this conversation. Our destination close now, I glanced at mine. Then I stared.

"Denise, let's skip our lockers and go to class," I hissed, forcibly turning her in the other direction.

"What is wrong with you, Samantha? I need my books."

"No, you don't, just trust me. They'll let you share with someone." I started nudging her towards her second hour. She tried to object again. "Please!" I begged.

"Okay, okay!" She sighed furiously, but she kept moving in the direction I wanted.

I left Denise at her second hour, but instead of heading down to the kindergarten room for mine, I ducked into the girls bathroom and waited. When the bell sounded again, and the hallways cleared of kids, I slinked back to my locker. Taped to the metal door was a piece of notebook paper. Written on the paper in big, black magic marker letters were the words: QUEER LOVER. I tore it off, wadded it up, and stuffed it in the nearest trash can. With luck, no one who had seen it would realize it had hung from *my* locker.

Chapter Four

I didn't know who posted the sign on my locker. Any Weasel could have done it—Weasel being my new official term for anyone who called Mr. Dubois gay. And I wanted to smash them all—get all of them back for trying to humiliate me. No way, now, that I'd ever muster the courage to face any of them with Bobby's evidence. Not when I knew somebody was more than willing to embarrass me in front of my entire school. So, since I'd ruled out vindicating Mr. Dubois for now, my thoughts turned easily to petty revenge.

Yeah, any Weasel could have done my locker. But the Turkey Creek student body probably contained more Weasels than non-Weasels. Revenge on that scale outstripped practicality. Frank Stallinger stood out from the wriggling herd of suspects, however. Only Frank had personally confronted me, so far. Plus, he was mean as a snake. Billy Drake knew way too much of my and Denise's business for comfort, but he still worshipped Denise, and treated me decently because of it. Not likely he'd done the deed. No, Frank would be my main target.

The only question? *How?* I couldn't risk getting expelled. The vengeance should also be unrelated to the whole Dubois controversy, so Frank would have no idea who hated him. I wanted him to wonder, I wanted it to eat at his mind. Besides, if Frank didn't know, there'd be no reason for him—other than sheer meanness—to do anything *else* to me.

I sat trying to conjure up a plan one day when I witnessed a further example of Frank's meanness. His talent for torment ranged far beyond my single, small life. Denise and I occupied a concrete bench outside after eating lunch. Though I initially steered her away from the locker sign, I had since told her the details. She supported my desire to get Frank back, but she hadn't come up with any reasonable ideas either.

Anyway, I gripped the cement on either side of my legs, straining for a glimmer of diabolical genius. Denise tapped me on the shoulder. When I looked up, she discreetly pointed to our left. There Frank loitered with a few of his slimy friends, standing more or less in a circle around this girl.

"You're so ugly a dog wouldn't lick your face after you ate ice cream," Frank jeered.

"Yeah, you'd make Frankenstein scream!" one of his accomplices added.

She *was* ugly. But that didn't mean she deserved abuse. She probably had enough problems with *self-*criticism without Frank ripping at her. I got nauseous just imagining how she must hurt. Denise and I moved to another bench further away and sat down.

"Sam, I feel awful," Denise said.

"I know."

"No, I mean . . . I-I should have done something. Stopped him. But I'm afraid to," she admitted.

Oh, Denise. Grabbed by the guilts for not sticking up for a total stranger when I couldn't even scrape up the guts to defend Mr. Dubois. I wanted to slap her.

"It's all right," I managed to tell her. "Not worth it. I'm sorry for her too, but we don't even know her. Now, if she were your friend," I continued, swallowing hard, "then you could be ashamed. But for all we know, she might be an awful person. Maybe even a Weasel." I didn't really believe that. My next words, though, I did believe. "And if you'd said anything, Frank would have started on you next." Or me and Mr. Dubois, just because he noticed me with her.

We both stayed silent for a while. I returned to plotting evil against Frank. I glanced back over to where he stood. The girl had escaped somehow, and I jumped a little when I saw Maria in her place, talking to Frank. I'd notified Maria of my "war" with Frank, though, coward-like, I had given her no reason for it. She didn't like him either, though, so seeing them together startled me all the more.

When Maria finished with Frank, she strolled over to Denise and me.

"You've associated with the enemy," I said, when she plopped down on my other side. I'd made an appropriate distance between myself and Denise, but Maria didn't worry much about personal space.

"Huh? Oh, yeah, Frank," she laughed. "I don't know what got into me."

"Neither do I," I answered, wrinkling my nose. "Did you see him torturing that poor girl?"

"No, I just got here. Sounds like Frank, though," Maria admitted.

"Well, if you go near him again, cuss him out for me."

"What did you have in mind?" asked Maria.

37

I whispered my favorite, most choice swear words. The next thing I knew, she ran to Frank.

"Denise, she's really doing it!" I hadn't meant for Maria to actually carry this out. Denise laughed. I wasn't so sure of the humor. I might be asking for more trouble.

"I did it," Maria announced when she reappeared.

"Just what exactly did you say?" I asked her.

"I said, 'Someone told me to call you a . . .'" she began.

"That's enough," I cut in. Fortunately, she hadn't mentioned my name, and Frank didn't appear to be looking over at us. He must not have figured out the source of the profanity. We all cracked up after Maria mimed her imitation of the look on Frank's face. Pure shock. Good. I wanted him to experience more of the same.

The same week, a rash of goofing off struck my sixth hour math class. In math, I filled a table along with Denise, our friend Lisa Chen, and a new girl named Kim. A deadly combination for Mr. Randolph, our teacher. We'd already driven him half-insane, so we started on each other. Denise and Lisa grew especially aggravating. For a while Kim and I had joined them in performances like turning Mr. Randolph's two-drawer file cabinet around next to his desk so he couldn't find the handles when he reached for them. The poor man finally threatened to lower our grades by a letter if we so much as touched that cabinet again. Now we had no one to torment but each other. I was quickly tiring of the whole thing.

One afternoon, Denise and Lisa began plastering each other with "kick-me-hard" signs. They really started getting on my nerves. Once was funny, but fifty or sixty times proved monotonous. Not to mention I began to be embarrassed to be seen with them.

"Why can't you two do something useful, like me?" I finally protested.

"What *are* you doing, Sam?" asked Denise, as Lisa slyly taped a sign to her back. I wanted to scream. I managed not to.

"I'm trying to figure out what we can do to Frank."

"We should hire a hit man," Denise answered, half-seriously. "You know, it's not a bad idea—Kim, stop staring at me, I don't mean guns. I mean, somebody could get him with one of these." She peeled off the sign Lisa stuck her with and swiftly taped it to Lisa's back.

"Might as well," I sighed. "Everything I can come up with would get us expelled. Well, who should we get to do it?"

"Why don't you do it yourself, Sam?" asked Kim. She couldn't help it. She was new.

Denise looked as if she was considering this, so I said quickly: "No. Then he'd know who's behind it. If he knows it's me, he'll know why I did it. I want him to be puzzled." Besides, if we did a whole series of these little stunts to Frank, and he couldn't find out the force behind it all, maybe I'd be able to make him as paranoid as I was.

"Whatever you say, Sam," agreed Denise.

I guess a kick-me-hard sign holds a certain *je-ne-sais-stupidity*, but I desperately wanted to pull *something* on Frank. Besides, I also made a solemn vow to myself. Given the right opportunity, I'd *really* get even. And taped-on signs would play no role.

But meanwhile, I had to pick out a hit man. Or woman. Finding the right person wouldn't be easy, though. Not only couldn't *I* tape him, but no known friend of mine could, either. Frank hadn't connected the incident with Maria to me only by sheerest luck— and his own stupidity. I couldn't take any more chances—even Frank's stupidity had limits. I think I managed to get the QUEER LOVER sign off my locker with minimum damage to my reputation, but I might not be so lucky with whatever Frank's next move might be. I couldn't afford to provoke him. Besides, like I said before, it's scarier to the victim if he has no clue who does it, or why.

So Denise and I concentrated for about a day on figuring out someone to do the job for us. By the next afternoon on the way home from Turkey Creek, though, we'd lost all seriousness. But then Denise nudged me. She pointed at the kid ambling along thirty feet or so in front of us. We both knew him, had known him since sixth grade. A seventh-grader named Jeremy Soames, who seemed all right, I guess. Denise always said he reminded her of a frog. After she first mentioned it, he reminded me of one, too. A boring, common green pond frog, but I never held it against him.

"Maybe Jeremy could get him for us," Denise whispered.

"Maybe you're crazed," I suggested. "You actually think we should go through with it?"

"Don't turn chicken on me now, Sam. After all the raving you've done about Frank?"

She was right. We went through with it. Luckily, Jeremy agreed for nothing, since we didn't have much money. No borrowing it, either. Oh yeah: "Dad, I need a loan to hire a hit man." Anyway, we informed Jeremy we'd have the sign for him the next day, and we'd meet him outside the north doors of Turkey

Creek. Jeremy would get Frank during their shared first hour—another piece of luck.

But Denise and I had hired the sloppiest hit man since the first amoebas sloshed aimlessly through the earth's oceans. After first hour, Jeremy reported he hadn't completed the assignment because the tape wouldn't stick. By lunch, he still hadn't succeeded. We told him to keep trying. Maybe Jeremy did, but he never got Frank. As far as we know, Frank never noticed the attempts, either.

I got Frank, though, the day after. Well, Denise helped me. And not a kick-me-hard sign in sight. I sat in third hour science, extremely bored. Lisa, who had the same class, didn't show because of flu. Kim, who had the class too, did show, but busily worked on her science project. No one to talk to. The urge to work didn't show either, at least not for me, so instead I asked Mr. Balsam for a library pass. I planned to go there and goof off. Of course, I had enough brains not to tell him that. I "needed to go do more research" for my own science project. He let me go. I'll be forever grateful.

Denise met me there. She'd wrangled her own pass. Her third hour teacher had the competency of a sautéed zucchini, so Denise goofed off a lot. We made ourselves at home, talking to Ann, a library aide. Library aides had it great. They only had to help Ms. Bloch, who in addition to heading the French Club, ran the library at Turkey Creek. Easy enough. In exchange, they didn't have to endure gym class.

Ms. Bloch sent Ann to re-shelve some books across the room, then looked around. "I wish Celia had come today," she said. Celia was the other third-hour library aide.

"Why?" I asked her.

41

"Oh, there's this list I want compiled. I don't have time to do it myself. The names of all the seventh-graders who've signed up to become library aides next year need to be put together. Would you do it, Samantha?"

"Sure, Ms. Bloch." Every spring this happened. Sign-up sheets went up in all the seventh-grade first hour classrooms, and if you wanted to be a library aide, you scrawled your name on it. I would have signed last year, but I tried to get into the Eighth Grade Chorus with Bobby instead. With my voice, I didn't make the cut.

Ms. Bloch wanted me to enter the names from all the separate sign-up sheets into one big alphabetized list on the computer. I sat down to do this in the chair Ann had occupied. Denise looked over my shoulder at the lists I started to shuffle. I skimmed through the sheets, scanning all the names. I would leave Turkey Creek forever in June, but I still wanted to see who next year's library aides might be. A particular name riveted my attention. To Denise's—and my own—surprise, I growled. I actually growled. The name, of course, belonged to Frank Stallinger.

I began the list, typing the names in slowly and carefully. Eventually I finished the *R*'s and started on the *S*'s.

"This is awful," I hissed at Denise. Then I growled some more. "I don't want to pollute this computer file by entering that Weasel's name. He shouldn't even be considered, but what can I do?"

"Simple," said Denise. "Leave him off the list."

"Really?" I whispered, in awe of the idea. "Could I? I *could!* But should I?"

"Beats sitting here growling at it," Denise answered.

She had a point. In a minute the deed was done. Or *not* done, more precisely. Frank would not be a library aide next year if all went well. Denise and I felt extremely proud of ourselves—she for thinking of it, and I for having the guts to carry it out.

When the list I made got printed out and copied for distribution among the teachers to make sure no one not on it tried to attend the special meeting for the final selection, I swiped a copy. Sure enough, Frank's name was glaringly absent. Oh, such fun! Picturing him trying to convince whatever teacher he had that hour: "There has to be some mistake!" What an amazing feeling! And what a shame Denise woke up sick that morning so I couldn't share it with her. The joy tasted just too good, sweet, and chocolate to savor alone. I saw Bobby striding past in the hallway. Before fear stopped me, I reached out and grabbed his hand, drawing him into a convenient doorway.

"Look at this!" I yelled, waving the list in his face. I had discussed Frank with Bobby, and he agreed the boy gave scum a bad name, even though I hadn't specified why I disliked the Weasel. I had even confided what Denise and I had done to the library list. So Bobby knew what I showed him.

"Sam Gabreaux—who'd have thought *you* would do something like this?" He smiled at me, like he thought me amusing or something. "Good job, Sam."

Denise reacted even better than Bobby when I called her up after school. Unfortunately, our joy flew only long enough to cause severe anguish when it crashed. About a week after the list got printed up and the meeting held, Mr. Dubois announced he'd heard Frank would be moving soon. The news produced mixed emotions in me. Gladness and relief to be rid of him—I'd never have to worry anymore about him trying to ruin my life. Part of me sprang suddenly free after a long time in a dark dungeon. But only part of me. The other part agreed with Denise about the bitterness of our library list efforts being in vain. Also, when Frank moved, he'd be beyond reach of any further revenge. Even if I dared risk the shrieked accusations, I couldn't beat him up on the last day of school—the only day I probably wouldn't get expelled for it. Despite our relative sexes, I'm sure that physically I could have caused Frank serious harm. My height gave me a better reach, and Frank's thinness did not make him wiry. But with his departure approaching, I feared I'd never really finish with Frank. I doubted I'd ever break the hold he had on me.

On his last day, though, I decided to be festive. I wrote this in my diary:

"Today, my least favorite person in the known universe, Frank Stallinger, has moved. Never again will I hear his sickening voice talking about Mr. Dubois. I am unkind to write these next lines, but he deserves no kindness from me.

"I hope, wherever he goes, he gets exactly the same comments he so eagerly heaped on Mr. Dubois, even though I have remained above doing this to him myself. There's an extremely good chance of it happening, what with his small, slender body and that thin voice of his. As a new kid somewhere else, he will be especially vulnerable. Probably won't be *true* when they say it—so much the better. He'll find out just what it's like, and maybe—just maybe—he'll learn his lesson."

I meant every word I wrote, but I was wrong about never hearing his sickening, thin voice again. I heard it in my head all the time.

Chapter Five

By the time Frank moved, spring had become definite. I had long since finished *The Lord of the Rings*. Parts of it lingered in the back of my mind though, and I even had a strange dream once, connected to the books. In the dream I was the other Sam and yet still me. I stood on a high, grassy hill—something like Weathertop in the trilogy—and I looked down at Turkey Creek Middle School. Kinda weird, because the only thing resembling a hill near Turkey Creek is the terribly worn-down pitcher's mound of the softball diamond. But in the dream I topped a hill. I held a shimmering silver sword high above my head, and the sword glinted in the light of a full moon. The only sound came from the howling wind, but the wind didn't scare me in the least. Instead, it whipped deliciously cool against my face. My heart beat fast, and I thought it might explode inside of me—I felt more free than ever before. I looked to the sky. Thousands upon thousands of brilliant stars shown against the blackness, and I laughed wildly, unable to contain my joy any longer. I could do anything. Me! Courageous! I bounded down the hill, sword still raised. I moved as powerfully and gracefully as a wild deer, leaping and landing again effortlessly. I ran towards the school building, shouting, "I have returned, Weasels, and I am victorious!"

I woke up with unusual longing afterwards. The longing came back whenever I remembered the dream, and I'd wish I could be like that for real. I think it tied in with Frank's leaving before I could face up to him. His moving frustrated me, reduced my list-altering to dust. Maybe that's why I started wanting revenge on Billy Drake. My worst Weasel escaped my vengeance. My second worst would not—not if I could help it.

Speaking of Drake, while reading *The Lord of the Rings,* I discovered some parallels between people I knew and characters in the story. If I considered myself to be like Sam Gamgee (only not nearly as brave), then Billy Drake made a natural Gollum. Not a nice thing to say, and I don't mean the part about Gollum looking like a concentration camp victim because Drake was puffy, but it was true. They shared the same *slimy* quality. Plus, Drake always acted awfully nice to Mr. Dubois when the man was around, but when Mr. D. went out of earshot, he'd start muttering about how sick it made him to be near "that queer." For those who haven't read the books, or seen the movies, backstabbing was a typically Gollumish trait. I wanted to choke Drake.

Funny. When I'd read about Gollum, I'd felt sorry for him. The desire for the Dark Lord's ring twisted him, and he couldn't help his horrible ways. But I didn't feel the least bit sorry for Drake. Oh, part of me knew I'd be no better than him if I hadn't started talking to Mr. Dubois again, but I didn't care. If I could keep myself from stooping so low, Drake should, too. He deserved whatever problems Denise and I could give him.

I sometimes wondered if Mr. Dubois realized Drake made all these remarks behind his back. At first I didn't think so. I figured Mr. Dubois for a complete innocent who wouldn't believe me if I told him. But then I wondered some more. In *The Lord of the Rings,* Frodo knew about Gollum all along. His kindness prevented him from doing anything about it, and eventually Gollum betrayed Frodo and Sam. I decided finally that Mr. Dubois resembled Frodo. He knew, but the size of his spirit didn't allow him to hold it against Drake. I had no such handicap. I hated the little Weasel all the more for that reason.

As with Frank, Denise figured out our revenge against Drake. She did it by accident one day while we ate lunch together in the school cafeteria. We talked of Weasels in general—not exactly unusual these days. We talked of Drake in particular—not exactly appetizing.

"The creep is still madly in love with me," Denise complained. "It's enough to make me puke." I couldn't argue with either point. Drake's crush on Denise, which had lasted about as long as I'd been in love with Bobby, never sank far from the surface. To Denise's credit, she avoided open cruelty to Drake, but she definitely didn't encourage him, either.

"He makes me want to puke, too," I agreed. Then an odd thought came to me. "But you know," I told Denise, "I wish he loved me instead of you."

"For God's sake, why?" Her face resembled that of a rich, cultured woman who had just stepped in a huge pile of dog crap.

"I'd break his heart," I replied. "I don't care how stupid I'd look, I'd flirt with every other guy in sight.

Especially ones even uglier and wimpier than him. Just to show him what a worthless thing he is."

"Yeah, right. Like you'd do anything like that in front of Bobby," said Denise. "But it's not a bad idea. Maybe I'll try it sometime when I'm bored." She started laughing about it. Then she couldn't stop. She sounded pretty hysterical. Probably just imagining Drake groveling at her feet, but I still shivered a little.

"Cut that out," I snapped. "You want somebody to think you're high?"

After a few seconds, Denise's eyes changed—alertness sprang into her pupils. She stopped laughing. "Oh! Oh, Sam! That's it!" she exclaimed in a loud whisper.

"What's it?"

"We can make Drake think I'm on drugs! That'll scare him half to death!"

"Do you think he'll bite?" I asked. My grin at her probably stretched as wide as Bobby's grin when he told me about Mr. Dubois and Ms. Evans.

"Drake? He'd bite if you told him Hitler won the Nobel Peace Prize," said Denise. "Besides, haven't you got a reputation for . . . well, no one would ever suspect *you* of playing a trick like this. Especially not somebody as stupid as Billy Drake."

I didn't know exactly how the goody-goody reputation had stuck to me—probably unnecessary civility to teachers. For once, my good behavior would come in handy.

We did it, and, if I must say so myself, fantastically. Denise acted all giggly and weird whenever she thought Drake might be watching her. If I happened to be with her at the time, I'd pretend to give her a stern warning. Academy Award material, definitely. Denise giggled so well I almost wondered if maybe she hadn't experimented with a few joints to gain realism in performance. As for me, I read once that actors do a much better job if they imagined the things they presented really happening. I have a good imagination. We had only to wait for a chance to find out if Drake was buying our act.

We didn't have to wait long. The clincher came in Mr. Dubois's room. A few days after Denise started her giggling, we went to see him after sixth hour. Drake stopped in to ask Mr. Dubois about homework. I paced near the chalkboard, restless. Denise leaned on Mr. Dubois's desk, talking to him. When Drake sauntered into the room, with his weird gait, I recalled something Maria had said about him once: "That kid walks like he's pregnant." I noticed Denise managing to give Drake one of her spaced-out stares without Mr. Dubois catching it.

My hands started to sweat as Drake waddled towards me. In a flash I knew whatever I said to him would be crucial in pulling this stunt off.

"She's crazy," said Drake, casting a meaningful glance in Denise's direction.

"Not only that," I muttered darkly, supposedly to myself but just loud enough for Drake to distinguish my words. I pretended to study the uninteresting beige tile covering the floor. Hopefully I'd be able to start laying it on pretty thick any minute.

"What?" Drake asked, nibbling the bait.

"N-nothing!" I stammered, as fearfully as I could. I tried to make myself look as if I had something to hide. No problem. With all the Dubois stuff I'd been through, I'd had plenty of practice.

"Something *is* wrong, *isn't* it, Samantha?" he asked, almost triumphantly. I swore he'd feel no triumph by the time I finished.

"No, Drake, I don't know what you're talking about!" I said desperately. Then I drew in my breath with a quick gasp, and let it out with a slow, heavy sigh. "Oh, why bother?" I mumbled. "I won't be able to keep it from you much longer anyway." To Drake's complete bewilderment, I dragged him into a corner of the classroom and threw a quick, furtive glance in the direction of Denise and Mr. Dubois.

"What's going on, Samantha?" Drake asked.

"She's high!" I hissed softly. He looked shocked. At least, his face whitened by two shades. "Honest," I added, for good measure. "She's been stoned every day for the past week or so!"

"She *has* been acting awfully weird lately," Drake agreed, gravely. *Idiot*, I thought. He actually believed me! I wanted to laugh in his face, but he never guessed it.

"You won't tell Denise I told you this, will you? And you won't tell anybody else?" I asked.

"Oh, no, Samantha!" he answered earnestly. "You can count on me to keep quiet. And if I can do anything to help, just let me know."

"Thanks. I'm really worried about her, Billy." I stepped over to where Denise was, said goodbye to Mr. Dubois, and we left. Mr. Dubois prepared to leave too, and Drake came behind him, all thought of homework apparently extinguished. Denise saw Drake staring at her and marked it with an insane giggle.

"Cut that out!" I whispered loudly, purposely remembering Drake's Gollumish qualities. "You want Mr. Dubois to find out?" I even slapped her—not hard—to make it look good. When we'd passed the point where our way home diverged from Drake's, I gave Denise the details of my conversation with him. We laughed a long, satisfied laugh.

The next Monday I accidentally-on-purpose met Drake in the halls. The kid's concern for "poor Denise" had led him to consult his family doctor about what might have caused "all this."

"Not by name or anything—I didn't get her in trouble," Drake assured me. "Anyway, he said most of the time people do drugs because they feel unwanted. Has Denise been feeling unwanted lately?"

"Well, come to think of it . . . ." I pretended to weigh the situation. "A week or so before she started, she complained about not being popular," I continued. God, my slickness! "You know, I bet that's the whole problem. I hear it happens a lot—you know, kids smoking joints and stuff so other people will like them. Awful," I sighed. "Just awful."

"You're probably right, Samantha," Drake agreed. "The best thing to do is to pay lots of attention to her, and show her she still has friends."

"I will, I guarantee," I said, gratefully. Actually, I had my suspicions Drake would strive to the best of his ability to make Denise feel wanted. Poor Denise. Aloud, I commented: "You're so helpful, Drake. I'm really glad I told you about this. It's just too much for me to handle alone." We parted company for our separate classes. When I ran into Denise, I repeated for her everything Drake had said. She chuckled gleefully.

I don't remember how long we went on, but while we did, we thoroughly enjoyed ourselves. I seriously considered taking up acting. For a while, anyway. Deep down I knew better. I'd never be able to do anything like what I did to Drake on stage or in front of a camera. This would be my last as well as my first great performance.

51

We didn't laugh anymore after we talked to Mr. Dubois. I don't know how the conversation got started. I don't know *why* it got started, either. I guess we were just so proud of ourselves we had to tell him what we were doing to Drake's little mind. Besides, we'd done it for *him*—Mr. Dubois, I mean.

"It's so amazing!" I exclaimed to Mr. Dubois. "The best part started right here in your room, that time Drake came in. He probably wanted to ask about an assignment or something. Well, I sure made him forget whatever he came for! You should have seen his face when I told him she was high!" I laughed, and Denise laughed with me, but Mr. Dubois didn't laugh. He just leaned against his desk, listening to us.

"You should see the way he looks at me now," added Denise. "Like I'm dangerous!"

"He's really going for it, then?" asked Mr. Dubois. But he didn't ask eagerly, enthusiastically. His tone remained even, with hardly enough inflection for a question.

"Yep," Denise and I said proudly. But my performance didn't please me quite so much anymore. Denise did a backwards Cheshire cat—everything else stayed while her smile slowly disappeared.

When we left him, nothing in Mr. Dubois's goodbyes sounded other than cheerful. But as we walked home, a dark suspicion grew larger in my heart. Mr. Dubois didn't approve of our making an even bigger fool of Drake than God had to begin with. Even though he hadn't *said* anything judgmental or disapproving, I couldn't shake my unease. Even thinking how much Drake reminded me of Gollum didn't work. If anything, it made things worse.

Denise didn't talk while these things ran through my head, and when I looked over at her, she seemed subdued, too.

"I feel guilty, Sam," she said suddenly. Took me by surprise. Denise never felt guilty over anything she did. Things she *didn't* do, yes, but . . .

"About Drake?" I asked, to make sure. She nodded. "I know what you mean," I confessed. "Ever since we told Mr. Dubois."

"Yep."

"But what can we do? How can we fix it?" I asked her, not sure I truly wanted an answer. "We *can't* tell Drake the truth."

"That would only hurt him more," Denise agreed.

"I guess we'll just have to tell him you're off the stuff," I said, giving in more fully to my guilt.

"Yeah. That'd be the best way. Maybe you can tell him I met some great guy at the YMCA who got me to give it up," suggested Denise. She swam at the Y sometimes after school as part of her parents' philosophy of constantly having her *do* things. The irony—they probably thought it would keep her off drugs.

"You know, we're just a couple of saps," I said, after we walked again for a few moments in our own separate thoughts.

"Yeah, I know."

We followed our new plan to the letter the next day. Or at least I did, since all Denise had to do was stop acting weird. Thankfully, Drake believed me. He looked sad about the guy at the Y, but relieved at Denise's "recovery." We'd managed to squirm our way out of that one with minimal damage.

I only stayed glad for roughly an hour and a half. Only that much time passed between my telling Drake

53

of Denise's miraculous "cure" and my wishing with every cell of my body I'd never bothered. At lunchtime, when Denise and I finished eating, we went outside for a while. We were sitting on our usual bench when Drake strolled up with Jeremy Soames. I almost ignored Drake's silly walk, felt almost willing to make peace with him, because it was too nice a day to hold grudges. Sunshine, blue sky, perfect temperature. Even Weasels look better in that kind of weather. Drake and Jeremy started talking to us, and we held up our end. Wouldn't you know it? We strayed onto the subject of Mr. Dubois. Denise and I should have been more careful and prevented this, but we didn't realize how the conversation drifted until way too late. Drake, of course, said things about Mr. Dubois he'd said many times before and would probably say many times again. And Jeremy agreed with him! After we'd trusted him with our sign! I glanced at Denise. She rolled her eyes at me. Drake rambled on and on. Something about how our parents should protest Mr. Dubois's presence in the school system. I boiled, but I still couldn't bring myself to say anything. Still too risky—there were lots of popular kids in the vicinity. Actually I didn't think *that* much about risk. Figuring out *why* took up too much of my mind. *Why* did we show him any mercy? *Why* did I tell him Denise dumped the dope when I knew deep down he didn't deserve it? *Why* is this always so? *Why*, if you show any kindness to a Weasel, do you regret it almost immediately? Arrrrgh! Instead of telling Drake that Denise had reformed, I should have had her ask him if he wanted to share a joint. A little late now, though.

I excused myself before fury and frustration exploded my head. Drake and Jeremy couldn't even scrape up enough brains between them to figure out they'd caused my departure—Denise told me later. Drake, at least, should have known. He should have realized by now that he didn't keep running into me in Mr. Dubois's room because I worked part-time as a bulletin board decoration. Just as well he was stupid. Denise wanted to follow me when I left—she told me that later, too—but she understood I needed solitude.

I sat down in the shade of the only tree in back of Turkey Creek. Many times last year in the seventh grade, I had sat beneath its welcoming branches, plotting out plans of action. The tree also made a good place to come at times like this one. From my shelter, I surveyed the schoolyard. Bobby loped nearby, throwing a football around with a bunch of other popular boys—boys who'd probably call him crazy if he ever asked me out. Especially if Weasels started publicly ridiculing me again for talking to Mr. Dubois. And Bobby would probably listen to both these boys and the Weasels. Who, having once attained good social standing in middle school, would give it up for someone like me? My situation seemed bad enough now, but I couldn't bring myself to make it worse by sticking up for Mr. Dubois. Not even to a wimp like Billy Drake. Any Weasel—not just Frank—knew how to make signs for people's lockers.

At least Bobby himself was no Weasel. I leaned my back against the rough trunk of the tree and studied my love for a while without his noticing me. I thought how nice it would be to paint him. He'd be such a good subject, but I lacked the artistic ability to make the picture anywhere near as beautiful as him. Maybe nobody could, and Bobby was a work of art in himself. I didn't really know. I just knew a little peace came from watching him.

The bell rang, signaling the end of lunch. I got up, sighed, and trudged into the building. I'd probably never get truly even with Drake, and my brief acting career had now finished. I tried to comfort myself with the knowledge Drake really *had* been fooled, even if only Denise, Mr. Dubois, and I knew. And Maria. After her remark about him walking like the pregnant, I couldn't resist telling Maria what we'd done to Drake.

Chapter Six

We let Drake off the hook too soon, and Frank had
completely escaped our vengeance. Alone, each of
these facts sat like lard in my stomach. Together, they
really cramped me. So much so that I finally decided
to sink to the Weasels' own level. Until now I'd
scrupulously avoided calling them the same names
they called Mr. Dubois, except for some private
speculations on the subject with Denise. But now—
now I wanted to lose all honor.

The week after Drake rubbed our mercy in our
faces, I left first hour and headed for the girls
bathroom, pencil in hand. I figured I'd hit a girls room
after each class. I chose pencil because spray paint
equaled expulsion, and my parents would have to pay
to have it stripped or covered. And people still read
pencilled graffiti—I knew *I* did.

I waited until I had the lavatory to myself. I knew I
had to be short and to the point in order to be effective.
Yet "FRANK SUCKS" didn't quite hit the mark. So I
scribbled, in big letters on the puke-green wall
opposite the stalls: "FRANK STALLINGER DIDN'T
MOVE. HE'S AT HOME DYING OF AIDS."

I knew I'd made another futile gesture. Frank would never know, would never hear the kids buzzing his alleged shame. But if it worked, *I'd* hear them, and I'd glory in it. A form of justice, anyway. And if Billy Drake didn't watch his mouth, he'd be next.

I'd managed to redecorate the bathroom in plenty of time to get to second hour in the kindergarten room. A little shaky from my deed, I looked forward to seeing Mr. Dubois on the way. The sight of him would strengthen my resolve, remind me of why I was defacing school property. But when I got to his classroom, a substitute slouched bewildered at the desk, leafing through Mr. Dubois' day-planner. Drake happened to be lounging by the door.

"Hello, Samantha!" he sang out. "Have you heard?"

"Heard what, Drake?" I grumbled.

"Mr. Dubois is in the hospital. I heard a couple of other teachers talking about it."

"Oh, my God! What for?" For a moment I forgot Drake's Gollum status, forgot I shouldn't show him my concern for Mr. Dubois.

"I don't know. I sure wonder, though, don't you?"

There—that slimy, insinuating tone again. And I'd had just about as much of it as I could take. "Oh, right, Drake!" I snapped. "I'm sure he's hospitalized because he's finally succumbing to AIDS like the queer he is!"

Drake's eyes widened at my vehemence. Then they narrowed again, an ugly slyness stealing over his face. "I bet you're exactly right, Sam," he said.

I turned and started swiftly striding to the kindergarten room, cussing under my breath. I'd done it this time. The solid fact I cared about Mr. Dubois had finally penetrated Drake's gelatinous brain. And now that he'd seen my weakness, never mind I was

Denise's best friend. Never mind he thought I'd confided in him about her "drug problem." He'd seen my weakness, and he would pick it like a scab, just because it was there. Or was it Mr. Dubois's scab he'd pick, no matter that mine overlapped it?

After second hour, I went in search of Ms. Evans. She stood outside her classroom, watching the hallways, like teachers throughout the universe did.

"He has pneumonia," she replied.

"Will he be all right?"

"Oh, yes," she assured me.

"Can Denise and I go visit him in the hospital?" I asked her.

"Maybe in a couple of days, when he's stronger. He'd probably like that. But not now—he needs to rest."

"Ms. Evans, I... I, well, I don't mean to be nosy, but will you see him tonight?"

"Yes, Samantha," she answered, smiling at me. "I'll tell him you said hello."

I thanked her and went off to third hour.

By lunchtime, everybody seemed to know Mr. Dubois was in the hospital, though *I* hadn't told anybody but Denise. And worse, they didn't know the truth—he suffered from pneumonia. Instead they whispered about various AIDS-related illnesses. Damn Drake! But for all I knew, maybe some of them *did* speculate about pneumonia. Pneumonia finished off more AIDS victims than anything else. Even the *facts* didn't make Mr. Dubois look better.

A cold, heavy weight squashed my chest. Maybe it was true. Maybe he did have AIDS. I forced myself to remember how he'd looked at Ms. Evans, forced myself to think about Bobby's evidence. But you didn't have to be gay to get AIDS. Mr. Dubois could've contracted it from sleeping with too many women. How ironic!

"My God," I said to Denise when she returned to the table after buying another carton of milk. "He could die!"

"Who?"

"Mr. Dubois," I whispered.

"Don't tell me you're starting to believe this stuff, Sam!" She sat emphatically down in her chair.

"Well, he *does* have pneumonia, and you don't have to be gay to get AIDS."

"Yes, but the only reason any of these kids think he *has* AIDS is that they think he's gay. Get a grip, Sam!" She was right, of course. Turkey Creek had become too weird for me to think straight—pardon the pun. Meanwhile, Denise kept raving. "That damn Drake! I wish I could just squeeze his head until it popped like a zit. Of course, I wouldn't want to use my own hands. Maybe a couple of bricks."

I suspected Drake's role in this chaos, but I asked Denise how she knew. "Well, he bounced right up to me and announced Mr. Dubois was in the hospital with AIDS," Denise answered.

"He didn't say where he got the info, did he?" I asked cautiously.

"No. I bet he made it up himself."

I didn't have the heart to tell her he'd had help, however unwitting and unwilling. In addition to the trauma of finding out Mr. Dubois was seriously ill, I had to deal with the knowledge that *I* was partially responsible for the latest terrible rumor about him. I couldn't punish Drake for something mostly my own fault. And I didn't dare do anything that might make the situation worse—though how it *could* get worse, I feared to imagine. After school, I made my way back to the girls room I'd decorated that morning. When I had privacy, I erased what I'd written about Frank. If I left it there, if too many people saw and discussed it, someone was bound to say Frank had gotten AIDS from Mr. Dubois.

For the next couple of mornings I went right to Ms. Evans's room when I got to school. On the third day she finally decided it'd be okay for me to visit Mr. Dubois in the hospital. Denise had another one of her countless lessons after school—I think tap dancing this time—so I decided to go alone. The hospital where Mr. Dubois recuperated happened to be well within biking distance of my house. I had been born there.

The hospital rules presented the only problem. You had to be sixteen years old to visit any patients other than maternity—apparently, this had slipped Ms. Evans's mind. Well, I'd just have to make sure I looked so old they wouldn't question me. For once my height would prove more asset than liability. But I still needed help.

When I got home, I peeked through the doorway into the kitchen. My mother was focused on preparing dinner, taking all the ingredients for her special chicken casserole recipe out of the refrigerator and setting them out on the counter. I dashed for the other end of the house, where my and my parents' bedrooms stood opposite each other. I entered theirs instead of mine, and opened my mother's top dresser drawer. The Victoria Secrets bra factory exploded before my eyes. I selected a model well-padded in the bottoms of the cups, designed to push one's assets into spectacular cleavage. I dashed back to my own room, shutting the door behind me.

I pulled a box of summer clothes from under my bed. I hadn't unpacked it yet, but the weather was warm enough now on a regular basis to wear most of the stuff. Besides, one blouse in the box would be perfect for what I had in mind—a light, gauzy little thing I could tie at the midriff. I retrieved it, laid it on my bed, and then rooted through my bottom drawer until I unearthed my tightest pair of jeans.

I threw them down beside the blouse, then stripped down to my underwear. I even replaced my white cotton socks with knee-hi nylons.

I tried on the borrowed bra. I hooked it at the closest hook, but it still hung loose. Well, God had made safety pins for just such occasions. I located one on my dresser and managed to fasten it tightly enough. I adjusted the shoulder straps and surveyed the results in my dresser mirror. Not quite the look I was after. I opened my sock drawer and corrected the situation.

When I had the blouse on and tied under my newly-enhanced breasts, I put on the jeans, lying flat on the bed to zip them. I opened my closet door and studied my collection of shoes. I needed something sexier than sneakers, but I couldn't wear heels to ride a bike, now, could I? I wanted to look older, not more stupid. Finally I fished out a pair of shiny black flats.

Fortunately, I did not have to go back and borrow my mother's makeup. My own lay on top of my dresser. Heavy on the purple eyeshadow, heavier on the eyeliner and mascara. Lots of blush. And then, the finishing touch—a tube of lipstick I'd bought by mistake, thinking it a much lighter shade. Instead, it turned out to be what Turkey Creek students fondly refer to as "ho' red." Perfect. I applied it thickly, then stood back and examined the total picture.

Well, I definitely looked different. What would Bobby think if he saw me? Would he like it? Would it help him fall in love with me? Probably not. Of all the many girls Bobby had gone with since we started middle school, none could be described as the out-and-out slut type. But many had been well-endowed. Maybe if I kept the chest ensemble but just used my regular makeup.... Nah. No sense in promising something you ultimately can't deliver.

I tried to slip past my mother in the kitchen and out to the back room where I kept my bike. Oh well.

"Samantha, have you experienced a sudden growth spurt or do you have socks in your bra?"

Worse, Mom, I thought. *I have socks in* your *bra.*

"And while we're at it," she continued, "why are you made up like that? Invited to film a heavy metal video?"

"Remember, you said I could go visit Mr. Dubois in the hospital?"

"And you think shock therapy will help him recover?" Her eyebrows lifted up, signaling puzzlement.

"You have to be sixteen for a visitor's pass, Mom."

She eyed me critically, top to bottom. "I think you'll get in," she finally said. "One word of advice, though. I'm making this food just for you and your father. By the time you get back, I'll be at Cheryl's lingerie party and your dad'll be here. You may want to have ditched the makeup and the socks by the time he sees you."

My mother trusted me. Rock-solid evidence of my dull life.

I pedalled over to St. Joseph's Hospital. Guys in cars honked at me—must've been the outfit. No convenient rack in the hospital yard, so I chained my bike to a telephone pole near the street. I adjusted my socks again before I entered the building and vamped up to the front desk.

63

"I'd like a visitor's pass to see Mr. Dubois," I murmured to the woman seated there.

"First name?"

"Samantha," I said, before I realized she'd meant *his*. The woman already looked like she didn't approve of me—now she thought me a complete idiot as well.

"Patient's first name."

I had to think for a moment. "Martin," I finally told her. "He's my teacher," I added, trying to explain my hesitation. Then I realized she might know Mr. Dubois taught *middle school*, and my cover might be blown.

"You don't look like the kind of kid who'd come to see a teacher," she commented as she scanned the patient files. *Fine*, I thought. *As long as I look like a kid who's old enough to come to see a teacher.* Aloud I said: "He's a very *special* teacher."

I don't know what she made of that last remark, but she located the pass for Mr. Dubois's room and gave me directions. I went up three floors in the elevator, and turned left when I got off, searching for room 439.

Despite Denise's firmness and my own wishes, my doubts still lingered. About whether Mr. Dubois had AIDS, I mean. I looked into the rooms I passed. The patients did not appear to be in isolation, and the town of Turkey Creek could not possibly have a whole hospital floor devoted to AIDS patients. That was another factor in Mr. Dubois's favor—Turkey Creek, Michigan, was way too small for great exposure to AIDS. Nothing like San Francisco or New York. Perhaps my town's small size also accounted for the relatively high percentage of immature Weasels I had to deal with. Still, one never knew.

I found 439. The door open, I peered around the corner into the room, which contained two beds—one unoccupied. Mr. Dubois was propped up in the other, reading a sailing magazine. Maybe not having anyone else in the other bed meant they'd isolated him. Then again, maybe the hospital just didn't have enough customers. Mr. Dubois wore one of those green hospital gowns, and tubes looped over his ears and met under his nostrils before becoming a single line. This line trailed down the side of his bed before turning up and leading into the wall behind him. Oxygen. A little pale, but otherwise Mr. Dubois looked okay. I stepped into the room and announced myself with a loud, cheerful, "Hi!"

Mr. Dubois looked up from his magazine. First his eyes grew big and his jaw dropped, then he started laughing. Then he started coughing. And coughing.

Oh, God, I've killed him. I frantically scanned the room for something to buzz a nurse with. But before I could find it, he straightened himself out. His face had traded pallor for redness now, but he still managed to smile. "That's kind of a new look for you, isn't it, Sam?"

I glanced around furtively for hospital personnel as I dragged a chair over by his bed. "You have to be sixteen to visit here," I whispered.

I saw him strain hard not to start laughing again, but his smile stretched even bigger. "You went to all that trouble, just to visit me?"

"No trouble. Actually, it's kind of fun."

"Really, Sam, this is so nice of you!"

"Well, I worry. You *are* going to be okay, aren't you? I mean, Ms. Evans said so, but..."

"Yes, Sam. I'll be all right. I'll be back at school in a couple of weeks."

"Good."

I didn't know what to say next, so I tried to read his chart in an unnoticeable way. The only understandable thing on it read "pneumonia." But maybe they didn't come out and say AIDS on a patient's chart.

"So, how's Denise?" asked Mr. Dubois, breaking the silence.

"She's fine. She would've come with me, but she had tap dancing."

"And how's Bobby?" he asked, in a teasing tone somebody my own age would use.

"Okay, I guess. No new developments," I reported.

A nurse came into the room. She eyed me strangely, but didn't say anything, except to Mr. Dubois. "Time to draw some more blood."

"You mean I've got some left?"

She made a little *hmmmphf* noise at him, starting the procedure as soon as he offered up his arm. She did everything very carefully, putting on a pair of rubber gloves first, but maybe they followed this procedure with all patients. When she left, I said, "So, you've got pneumonia." Brilliant, I know.

"Yeah," said Mr. Dubois. "I first caught it when I was about your age, and after you get it once, it's fairly easy to get it again. You know, like Elizabeth Taylor."

That his pneumonia was recurrent since his teens pointed away from AIDS. But I still worried. Mom kept up on all that Hollywood stuff, and I knew Elizabeth Taylor had almost died from *her* pneumonia.

Eventually I had to tell Mr. Dubois that my dad was probably waiting supper for me. After I handed my pass back to the woman at the front desk, I found a public restroom. I washed all my makeup off with wet paper towels, but then I was stuck. I don't like carrying a purse when I ride a bike, so I had nowhere to put my socks if I took them out of the bra. Oh well.

66

I had plenty of socks at home. I almost tossed them in the garbage, but then I decided to leave them out on the counter by the sinks. Maybe a homeless person would come in and find them.

Even without the socks, the bra added a little bit more than natural. But I untied my shirt and buttoned it normally, which created a much looser effect. Of course my pants still squeezed like cling wrap, but I *did* wear them occasionally, anyway. I could face Dad now.

He met me as I put my bike away in the back room. "I was just getting ready to eat without you," he told me cheerfully, already out of his postal uniform and into his evening attire of jeans and t-shirt. "Your mom's at some kind of frilly underwear party, but she left us a casserole."

"I know," I said. I sat down with him to steaming plates of my mother's special chicken and cheese recipe. Not long after we had finished it, and my father had settled himself in front of an old Clint Eastwood western while I had my nose in one of my mother's more *educational* romance novels, the doorbell rang.

"You want to get that, Sam?" my father asked.

Not particularly, but with my mother gone, I automatically became the most outgoing person in the house. "Sure," I sighed, dropping the book and crossing to the door. I used the peephole. A thin, slightly balding, dark-haired man waited on our porch; at his side stood a shorter, somewhat wider, dark-haired woman. Both wore dignified clothing. From encounters at various parent-teacher conferences, I recognized them as Bobby's parents. What were *they* doing here? Hoping I looked all right, I opened the door and beckoned them into the living room. "Daddy, this is Mr. and Mrs. *Bouchard*," I told my father. I hoped he'd understand the emphasis I put on the last name, realize these were Bobby's parents, and not do or say anything to embarrass me. "This is my father, Joseph Gabreaux," I said to our guests, as they seated themselves on the sofa.

"Young lady," Mrs. Bouchard said to me, "if you don't mind, we would like to speak to your parents alone."

"My mother's not here," I said, backing out of the room. I felt myself blushing. They didn't even know my name—apparently Bobby never talked about me at home. But honestly, had he ever given me any reason to think he had?

I left the room all right, but I definitely wanted to know why they'd come here when they didn't even know us. I sat down in the hallway where they couldn't see me, but where I could still hear everything.

"Well, we'll just have to make do with you, Mr. Gabreaux," said Mrs. Bouchard.

"What can I do for you?" my father asked. I could tell from his voice he struggled to be polite in the face of Mrs. Bouchard's condescension.

"We're going around to parents of Turkey Creek Middle School students and alerting them to a situation that has come to our attention," Mrs. Bouchard continued. Mr. Bouchard must just be there for decoration, I decided. "Your girl, the one who let us in. She looks about the right age; she *is* a student at Turkey Creek?"

"Yes," replied my father. He was probably cursing me silently for letting them in.

"Well," Mrs. Bouchard began, "are you aware that one of Turkey Creek's teachers, someone your daughter may come in contact with *daily*, is probably a flagrant homosexual suspected of carrying the AIDS virus?"

She had to mean Mr. Dubois! By God, if Billy Drake had appeared suddenly before me at that moment, I'd have choked every last breath of life from him! This had to have started with *his* parents. They'd probably be the only adults stupid enough to take his ravings seriously. Besides, hadn't Drake already mentioned that his dad kept threatening to do something like this? Yet, I was to blame now, too. I provided the rumor, the one that must have pushed his dad over the edge. Drake hadn't imagination enough to do it alone. And what about Bobby? Did he know what depths his folks had sunk to? He *had* to. But why hadn't he told them about seeing Mr. Dubois and Ms. Evans out together?

"A group of concerned parents is meeting at the community center a week from Friday to discuss the issue of this teacher, Mr. Dubois, and what action should be taken against him," said Mrs. Bouchard.

"Wait a minute," said my father. "What evidence do you have?"

"Apparently the entire student body is talking about it," began Mrs. Bouchard.

"All the kids are *talking* about it?" my father repeated. "On *this* basis you want to get a meeting together?"

"Where there's smoke, there's fire. Can we count on you and your wife's support?"

I heard the sound of my father rising from his recliner.

"No, you may not," he said quietly. "You may also leave now, and might I also suggest that you and your husband get a life?"

I didn't know whether to cheer or to scream in frustration. If by some miracle Bobby ever did fall in love with me, relations with his family would not be good. After the Bouchards left, my father called me back out to the living room.

"Did you hear all that?" he asked me.

"Yes, Daddy."

"I thought so. Now I want you to hear *me*. You might not think I pay attention to what goes on in your life, but I do. I know who Mr. Dubois is. I know you and your mother think the world of him. Fine. But you're not to mention any of this to your mother, you understand? Because if she finds out, she'll make me put on a suit like that poor, silent jerk who was just in here, and drag me to that damn meeting to fight for Mr. Dubois. Trust me, Sam. It'll all blow over without our help, and I'll be a lot happier if it does. You got this, Sam?"

"Yes, Daddy." Not only did I understand, but I knew he'd given me a good excuse not to tell my mother about this mess. I only hoped he was right about the blowing over part.

Chapter Seven

The next morning at Turkey Creek, I occupied my usual bench outside the front entrance when Denise showed up, hyper as anything. I knew the evil source of her energy, so I dragged her out of anyone's earshot before I let her tell me.

"Sam, you're not gonna believe this. Wait'll you hear what Drake has gone and done now!"

Just in case I didn't already know, I asked her to explain.

"He's gotten his parents in on this whole thing with Mr. Dubois," she told me. "They showed up at our house last night, trying to get mine to come to this meeting they're having to decide what to do."

"Are your folks going?" I asked.

"You bet. They're going to go defend Mr. Dubois!" Denise exclaimed. "Do you think yours will come?"

"No." I told her we'd had visitors with the same mission last night, and that my father had sworn me to secrecy.

"Too bad. Mr. Dubois needs every friend he can get," said Denise. She paused for a moment. "You mean Drake's folks got all the way to your neighborhood last night?"

"No. Some other parents." I didn't want to identify them, so I changed the subject. "Did the Drakes say much about their intentions with this meeting? Dad kinda cut our visitors off last night."

"Yeah, they want to get a hearing from the school board and demand Mr. Dubois be tested for the HIV virus," answered Denise.

Not so bad, I thought. He could just take the test, and when he passed, everything would be okay. I said as much to Denise.

"But he shouldn't have to!" she protested. "It's wrong! No, Sam, I'm stopping this dead. I'm talking to Drake at lunch and making him call his parents off."

I knew when Denise reached this mood, no one could call *her* off. I hoped she would succeed. But I didn't want to be anywhere near her when she confronted Drake. I couldn't quite let myself be associated with Mr. Dubois's defense—even though I had helped cause this latest problem. Though Drake, at least, must know how I felt by now, who knew who else might be listening when Denise gave him a piece of her mind? And since Bobby hadn't cared enough to correct his own parents about Mr. Dubois, I sure couldn't count on *him* to take my side against the Weasels.

So I dreaded lunch as Denise and I separated to go to our respective first hours. Speaking of Bobby, he proved uncommunicative in social studies. He just grunted at me when I said "hi," and he didn't turn around once the whole hour to ask me a question about our assignment. How did he discover my closeness to Mr. Dubois? What had he learned to warrant ignoring me to preserve his popularity? Well, maybe in a few years, when we'd all become comfortable in high school, people would have had long enough to forget the whole Dubois fiasco and Bobby could feel free to fall in love with me.

At lunch I meandered through the cafeteria first instead of sitting down with Denise right away. Silly, I know, because all my friends—except seventh-grader Maria, of course—sat at the same lunch table as me and her. I wasn't willing to give up their company permanently. Weasels could, and probably *would*, still associate me with Denise's bold move. But I had to try minimizing the damage.

So I lingered over by the trash compactor and watched Denise set her tray down beside Lisa and Kim. Ever efficient, she had apparently already seen Drake this morning and commanded him to appear at our lunch table. He showed up the moment she opened her milk carton. I didn't really want to get close enough to hear everything, but since I knew what to expect, I could tell what went on from gestures and occasional luck with lip-reading.

I can only describe the next few moments as weird. Instead of inviting Drake to seat himself, Denise rose to her feet. My best friend wore only loose jeans and a loose-fitting t-shirt. No makeup enhanced her, and she sported plain, round, spectacles. No objective person could've labeled her attractive that day. Yet the way Drake looked at Denise proved him as lovestruck as ever. She had some kind of power over him, some kind of power completely foreign to me. Unfortunately, she didn't hold this kind of power over any boy she actually *liked,* but she definitely held it over Drake. She started lecturing him. Her voice grew louder as she warmed to her subject, until I could hear: "It's not true, you made the whole thing up, and you'd better tell them and get them to stop." Drake just stood there taking it. *Good.* He might have protested *he* hadn't made it up—the idea sprang from *my* sarcastic remarks.

"If you don't," Denise continued, "if this meeting actually takes place, I will never speak to you again as long as I live, Drake!"

Drake looked like somebody had run over his dog with a semi truck. He had less chance of ever getting Denise to return his affections than I had with Bobby, and maybe he knew it, but it didn't matter. The threat of complete and total cut-off of any conversation still meant unimaginable hell. I understood. But he had it coming.

"You tell me they've called it off by tomorrow, Drake, or that's it," she finished. I waited for a few minutes after he slinked off to sit with Jeremy Soames, then I got my food and sat down with my friends.

The next morning, after I left Maria for Denise as usual, Drake came walking slowly up to us. His face made a Goth's look tanned, and his eyes had dark circles under them. I wanted to leave, but I didn't want Drake to realize he had the power to scare me. I also didn't want him to think I cared about his privacy with Denise. None of it mattered, not to Drake. He didn't even notice my presence.

"They wouldn't listen to me, Denise," he said quietly. "I told them I'd made it up, but they thought I was just embarrassed. They thought I was trying to get out of their attracting attention to me with their meetings. They asked why all the other kids said it if it wasn't true."

Denise just stood with her arms folded across her chest, staring at him.

"Denise, really, I tried! They wouldn't listen," Drake pleaded. "Don't be mad. I did my best!"

Denise said nothing, and while she said nothing, the bell announced first hour. She turned and walked swiftly toward the building, leaving Drake to stare after her like ... well, like I would've done with Bobby. Only he deserved it. Then he saw me.

"Sam, you have to get her to talk to me again!" He stepped in front of me so I would've had to touch him to go into the building.

Oh, right. Like I'd ever throw him a dead rat if he was third-world starving. I wanted to say something to that effect, but I remembered he could tell Denise *I* actually provided the source of the rumor. Not that she'd believe it if I denied it. But I decided it best to at least be civil, to seem a *little* sympathetic.

"You know Denise," I told him. "Once she makes her mind up, there's no changing it." I sidestepped him and headed for the door.

The next time I saw Denise, her focus had switched from Drake to Mr. Dubois. "You know, they didn't even invite him to the meeting so he could defend himself. Maybe we can't stop the meeting, but we can make sure he's prepared. We should go talk to Ms. Evans."

"No," I said. At first I didn't know why I objected, but as my thoughts sorted themselves out, I explained to Denise: "I want to be the one to tell him. I don't feel right having someone else do it, even though I'm sure Ms. Evans really cares about him. She shouldn't know before he does, you know?"

Amazingly, she followed my logic. "Yes, but Sam, the meeting is a week from tomorrow! We don't know when Mr. Dubois is coming back."

"Well, let's wait then," I said. "If he doesn't get back here by—oh, say, Wednesday—we'll tell Ms. Evans, okay?"

Denise agreed. Fortunately, Mr. Dubois did come back in time—Tuesday, as a matter of fact. Apparently, he bounced back from pneumonia better than the average victim of the disease. When I passed by on my way to the kindergarten room Tuesday morning, my gladness at seeing him almost made me forget to check and see who else was around. Students had virtually deserted the hallway—I'd been running kind of late. So first I congratulated him on being well enough to be back, and then I said I needed to talk to him after school.

Denise offered to come with me, but I told her I needed to go alone. Besides feeling I should do it because I was ultimately responsible—which I didn't tell her—I knew she'd want to go *right* after sixth hour. All sorts of people would still be wandering the halls. What with the upcoming meeting and the more serious rumors of AIDS, being seen voluntarily with Mr. Dubois had become more dangerous than ever. So I slipped into the girls room after sixth hour with a book, and waited. I knew Mr. Dubois would wait for me. Finally, when the lady custodian came in to clean the toilets, I figured I'd be safe. I went past her and her wheeled bucket, and headed for Mr. Dubois's room.

Sure enough, he remained. "I'm sorry I'm late," I said. I knew I should start off by telling him I'd caused everything, that my smart remark to Drake triggered the whole mess, but I couldn't. Not yet. Maybe everything would still be all right, and it wouldn't matter.

"Oh, that's okay, I've got stacks of homework to grade," Mr. Dubois answered me. "What's on your mind, Sam?"

I closed the door, and sat down in the middle desk of the first row. "You need to know something," I sighed. My voice stuck in my throat a little, but I managed to reveal the impending parents' meeting to him.

"I thought something was up," he said, after I'd remained silent for a moment. "In all the classes, the kids whispered among themselves. Not like normal — a lot more. And whenever I walked closer to them, they'd back away, shut up, and look guilty. Thanks for cluing me in, Sam."

"No problem," I said. "What are you going to do? I think everything'll be all right if you go to this meeting—it's at the community center—and tell them about you and Ms. Evans. And if they're real stubborn, just agree to take the test. Nothing has to go any further than this meeting—they probably won't go to the school board if you just agree to their demands."

When I finished, he got up and walked slowly to the front of his desk. He leaned against it and laughed, but the laugh sounded strange. If I had laughed when I found out Tina had told Bobby I liked him, it would have sounded something like that. "No, Sam," Mr. Dubois said quietly.

"W-w-what do you mean?" I sputtered. Icy fear crept into my heart again. I knew it was way too personal, I knew I shouldn't ask, but it just slipped out. "You *could* pass the test, *couldn't* you?" After I'd done it, though, I covered my mouth with my hand as if I could force the words back in.

"It's okay, Sam, I don't mind questions from you," he said, smiling at me reassuringly. "With all the times we've talked, I consider you my friend."

If he only knew. If he only knew I watched constantly to make sure no Weasels or no popular people hung around before I talked to him, and I'd kept him waiting this afternoon for the same reason. If he only knew I had accidentally started the mess now stinking around him.

"And because I know you are my friend, I will give you the truth," Mr. Dubois continued. "If you promise it will go no further. Not even if you think it will help me. Okay, Sam?"

"Okay," I said. I didn't know how I'd get away without telling Denise, but I promised anyway.

"I've already taken the test, and I'm happy to report I'm negative," said Mr. Dubois. "But I'm ashamed of why I took it."

Part of me wondered what Mr. Dubois could possibly have to be ashamed of. The rest of me guessed he'd tell me if I just stayed quiet.

"I got tested after my brother died. I'd taken a leave of absence to take care of him. I knew you weren't supposed to get it just from that, but towards the end .... I had to clean up so much. I took all the precautions, but I had to know. I felt like every ignorant jerk who shunned him during the last year of his life, but I had to know." The steadiness had never left his voice, but I saw the glimmer of water in his eyes.

"I'm sorry," I said. "I had no idea." Then, after a pause, I tried again. "But, it's not really anything to be ashamed of, and I'm sure if you just tell them..."

"You must think I'm crazy, eh, Sam?" His tone was gentle despite his words. "I know what they all say, and I know what things I do that provoke them. You must wonder, don't you, why I don't just stop waving my arms around when I talk, why I don't tone down the enthusiasm in my voice."

He knows? He knows what's causing all this and he still does it? My mind struggled with the concept. "If it was me," I admitted, "I would do anything to stop it. Not the parents' meeting—just the kids, talking."

"You know, Allan was like that too—like I am—but it had nothing to do with being gay or straight," he explained. "My whole family is very expressive, very open about emotion. I see no need to squelch a family trait just to keep people a good twenty years younger than me from talking—no offense intended, Sam."

"None taken. But still, all you need to do is explain all this to the committee, just like you explained it to me. And tell them about Ms. Evans, too, just to make sure."

Mr. Dubois sighed deeply. "Think about it, Sam. I told you these things because I wanted to. But they're none of your business, are they? They're none of anybody's business. I refuse to *use* my brother—or Ms. Evans—to keep my job. Besides," he continued, "if I did what they wanted, you're right—I'd probably be fine. But what about the next person? What happens to the next person they accuse? Some teacher here *could* turn up with AIDS someday. Should he or she lose his or her job because of it?"

"No."

"So you understand why I can't agree to this committee's demands?"

"Yes," I answered. "I don't know why you have to be so noble, but..."

"Noble!" Mr. Dubois laughed, but at least it sounded less bitter now. "If you say so. But enough about me—how are *you*, Sam?"

"Me? How am I supposed to be?"

He leaned closer to me, and his eyes were kind like my pediatrician when I'd had the mumps years ago. "I know this bothers you, Sam. I know you've been teased because of me, and I know you stopped coming by for a while because of it. I also know you hate a lot of the people involved. You won't do anything crazy, will you?"

I looked back at him, confused for a moment. Then I realized he was thinking about school shootings. I admit to being surprised it had never entered my head. My dad does have a lot of guns. I sat and thought about it a while before I answered.

"No, I won't," I told him. "As much hell as this place can be, as hard as it is for me to get away from it and remember there's something beyond it, I know things have got to get better eventually. If I pulled a stunt like that, I'd never know what my life would have been four years from now, eight years from now. Besides," I added, "I could never hurt you and Denise like that, let alone my parents."

"I didn't think so," said Mr. Dubois, smiling. "But I couldn't take the chance I was wrong."

I needed to get home before Mom and Dad got too worried, and Mr. Dubois decided to leave, too. As we exited Turkey Creek's front doors together, I asked him one last question:

"So, will you show up at their meeting at all?"

"No," he said. "They didn't invite me."

Chapter Eight

The parents' meeting took place. I kept my father's secret, so neither I nor any member of my family attended. Denise went with her folks, though, and reported back to me. Predictably, the majority of people at the meeting agreed that Mr. Dubois's teaching at Turkey Creek presented a problem, and they would take it up with the school board. About a week or so afterwards, Denise informed me it had been done. The school board had scheduled a hearing on the matter for the evening of the last day of school.

Meanwhile, other problems had developed. We had a new Weasel on our list. Well, actually several— what with the rumors intensifying so rapidly—but only one of them held enough interest to be worth mentioning. Denise and I hadn't met him, but we'd heard a lot, because the whole school buzzed over him. Timothy Lindy. He'd picked a fight with another boy right in Mr. Dubois's classroom. When Mr. Dubois tried to break it up, Timothy Lindy had deliberately turned around and actually *punched* Mr. Dubois!

Deep curiosity mixed with my fury. I'd never heard of a Weasel's going so far before—and he *was* a Weasel, on top of everything else. He'd called Mr.

Dubois a queer as he swung at him. I needed to know just what kind of psychotic personality we had to deal with. Who *was* this Timothy Lindy? Denise said she'd heard of him, and even I could say as much, but we could come up with little other information. I asked Lisa, who knew what he looked like, but she lacked good description skills. "Blond, blue-eyed, and terribly ugly," stretched most of her capabilities. Unfortunately, those words fit half the white male population of Turkey Creek. She also mentioned his height, but we had more than a few *tall*, blond, blue-eyed ugly boys, too. I asked her to point Timothy out to me, but he never seemed to be in the same vicinity as Lisa and me. I wanted to see him. I didn't think it wise to let a Weasel like Tim Lindy go unobserved. He'd actually *hit* Mr. Dubois!

One night not long after I'd learned of the incident, I called Maria. I tried to work my way towards the subject gradually.

"Maria, do you know a kid named Tim Lindy?" I eventually asked.

"Yes, and I know he hit Mr. Dubois, Sam, and that's why you want to know," Maria replied, sounding somewhat annoyed with me. So much for attempted nonchalance.

"Never mind that," I said. "What's he like?" I wanted to ask her when she'd become psychic, but I figured I'd get more out of her without sarcasm.

"He's not as bad as people say," answered Maria. "Everybody hates him, and he doesn't really deserve it. I don't know what's so awful about him. He seems all right to me."

I should have expected kind ol' Maria to defend someone she saw as the underdog, but I had my own ideas about who fit the label in this situation. I made some excuse to end the conversation. "Everybody hates him and he doesn't deserve it," I mimicked under my breath. "I bet his popularity got a good boost when he slugged Mr. Dubois." I was talking to the refrigerator, but apparently too loudly. My mother must have heard me hang up the phone first, because she called, "People who talk to themselves wind up in padded cells," from the living room. I didn't say anything more, but I concluded kids were already turning that Weasel into a hero for his actions. That Lindy had hit Mr. Dubois without worrying about dying if he'd drawn blood and had a cut on his hand apparently made people perceive him as even braver. A number of students—mostly girls—still didn't like Tim Lindy, but yes, his social standing definitely rose higher daily. Before I fell asleep that night, I pictured Frank pinning a medal on a tall, ugly, blue-eyed blond guy for "fighting queers in the school system." Stupid, judgmental Weasels.

Denise and I heard more about the "hero" the following Tuesday. Once in my life, back in the sixth grade of another school, I had loved Tuesdays. Our teacher had let us do all kinds of neat things on Tuesdays, like creative writing. Not so in the eighth grade at Turkey Creek—here, I dreaded Tuesdays. Denise and I had to operate the school cafeteria's radio station. Not a real radio station. They just called it one. The sound only reached the cafeteria, but that was bad enough. Denise had the brilliance to volunteer—I just went along with it to make her happy. We took a lot of abuse from hostile people who demanded we play such-and-such a song and threatened us with bodily harm if we didn't do it within the nanosecond. I really hated it. I hated it less when Denise showed up to field most of the insults, but a couple of times she'd been absent and I'd dealt with it alone. One of those times the Plexiglass protector separating me from the mobs in the cafeteria had fallen down. I thought I'd be ripped to shreds. After that, I decided to recruit a third helper in case Denise got sick on yet another Tuesday. The girl we got was new—nobody who'd been around awhile wanted the job. A seventh-grader named Rosalyn, but we called her Rose because she liked it better. As far as I knew, she met the non-Weasel requirement. She didn't even have Mr. Dubois for a teacher. But I really didn't know, and these days, I didn't want to ask.

On this particular Tuesday, all three of us showed up to do our painful duty. Painful for Rose and me, anyway. I started to eat my lunch, a turkey bologna sandwich, as Denise cued up the first record. I fell to thinking about our new Weasel again as I chewed.

"Rose, do you know a kid named Timothy Lindy?" I asked.

"Yes, and I wish I didn't," she muttered. "That kid is so *nasty*..."

"What do you mean?" asked Denise.

"Well, he's in my sixth hour class, and everybody hates him," said Rose. "At least, everybody halfway decent hates him. I swear, he can't go past a girl in the halls without grabbing at her butt."

"Charming," I said, wrinkling my nose. This was more like it. Rose's description sounded a lot closer to the kind of person who'd hit Mr. Dubois than Maria's had. Obviously, Rose knew him better. "And you've got him in your sixth hour? Rose, will you meet me outside Ms. Johnson's room after fifth? I want to go with you to your sixth. You can point Tim out to me."

She agreed, and when the time came, she quietly showed me Mr. Notorious. His blue eyes were pale and watery, and his face washed-out looking. I stared at him long and hard to make sure I'd remember him, just in case I ever had a chance to make him miserable. If I got some little chance, who could blame me if I took it? After all, he deserved punishment. Sure, he'd been expelled for a few days after he hit Mr. Dubois, but what was that? Not nearly enough—he probably enjoyed the time away from school. And as soon as they'd searched his locker and realized he wasn't keeping a diary plotting the death of the whole student body and staff, they'd let him come right back.

After I'd found out about the incident, I'd asked Mr. Dubois himself why *he* hadn't done anything. He admitted to me he'd wanted to, but decided the pleasure of popping Tim back didn't override the possibility of a lawsuit. Teachers have to be inhumanly careful as it is, and Mr. Dubois knew he already had enough trouble—even if he refused to do anything to help himself out of it. Oh well. If I ever saw the opportunity to slam Tim Lindy good—with little risk to myself—I'd snatch it in a heartbeat.

Not long after I'd identified the perp, my third hour science teacher announced he'd sponsor another afterschool horseback riding trip. Anyone from any of his classes could go. I loved horses, so I had gone on the first trip with Lisa, who also had Mr. Balsam for science. She and I decided to sign up again for the next time. A good afternoon of horseback riding would be perfect to take my mind off the whole Dubois situation—which also included Bobby, who still hadn't spoken more than one word at a time to me since his parents had shown up at our house.

I brought the horse rental money and permission slip in to Mr. Balsam as soon as possible. After I watched him put my money in with everybody else's,

Mr. Balsam asked me to sign the list of students going. The list hung on a clipboard tacked to the bulletin board, and from a habit I had developed in the library, I skimmed my way through the names. Tim Lindy's topped the others. I would go horseback riding with the infamous Timothy Lindy! Half of me sickened at the thought. For a minute I considered crossing his name out like I did with Frank's, but I decided against it. Mr. Balsam would have his permission slip, and he'd get to go anyway. Besides, it might be better to have Tim along on the trip. Maybe he'd fall off his horse and I'd trample him with mine.

Lisa, who kept forgetting *her* permission slip, still shared my views on Tim. "He lives in my neighborhood," she explained. "I never knew such a jerk could exist."

"In your neighborhood? Poor Lisa!"

"Yeah. But Sam, if you're ever up for revenge you could get plenty of help. Lindy has more enemies than anybody I know."

"I know someone who's got him beat," I muttered. And Timothy Lindy had scored a big hit—pardon the pun—with the enemies of Mr. Dubois. Weasels honored all the wrong things. I could probably become the most popular person at Turkey Creek if I copied Tim's act. Last thing I wanted to do, though.

I looked forward to the riding trip. Oh, I didn't seriously think I could hurt Tim, but who knew? Some unimagined golden opportunity might present itself in the course of the afternoon.

The day of the trip began well enough. At first, nothing out of the ordinary occurred. In second hour—I still helped in the kindergarten room with Bethany—we had visitors. Mr. Dubois sent a couple of seventh graders over with the guinea pigs he kept in his classroom so the little kids could see them. Apparently he'd pre-arranged this with Ms. Pole. Something about one of the girls who came over with the animals, something in her quiet politeness, made me say to myself she could not possibly be a Weasel. As much as anybody besides me and my closest friends could not be a Weasel these days, she couldn't. I didn't think much more about the visit—except to make a mental note to tell Mr. Dubois that, while the kindergartners had benefitted from contact with genuine rodents, I had not enjoyed cleaning up after his pets.

Things started to get weird at lunch, though. That's when I began to suspect the whole day would turn strange. Denise and I finished eating and walked outside. I wore a red-striped shirt. Renee Thompson sauntered towards us, and we braced ourselves. I classified Renee as the meanest female non-Weasel at Turkey Creek—or, as I said, what *passed* for a non-Weasel ever since the birth of the great AIDS rumor. She'd insult anybody she'd see, and I'd never heard her name and the word "nice" in the same sentence. People said she carried a knife in her pocket and knew how to use it.

"I've got a shirt just like yours at home," Renee said to me, quite pleasantly. "I like them, don't you?"

"Yes," I managed to get out, while Denise tried to put her lower jaw back in place.

"I don't believe it," Denise whispered, when Renee continued on. "I always thought she was a homicidal maniac, didn't you?"

"Yeah," I agreed. Then I got the funniest thought. "You know what I expect after this?" I asked her.

"An earthquake?"

"No. Something much more amazing," I assured her. "A nice, courteous letter from Frank Stallinger begging our forgiveness for every dumb thing he ever said about Mr. Dubois."

"After this, you just might get it," agreed Denise, chuckling a little. I laughed too, at the total impossibility.

Since so many of us planned to ride, Mr. Balsam had some other teachers help drive us over to the stables. I rode in the beat-up Chevrolet of some unknown math teacher named Mrs. Sands. I thought myself lucky to sit next to the same seventh-grade girl, Courtney, who'd been in the kindergarten room with the guinea pigs. We greeted each other, and I made myself comfortable, looking out the car window. I barely saw the scenery as I brainstormed ways to help Tim Lindy fall off a horse. Since Renee had spoken to me civilly at lunch, I mentally prepared myself for a day of total opposites from the ordinary. I even decided to enjoy whatever shocks might come my way—or Timothy Lindy's way, if my luck held.

But I definitely was not ready for what I heard next. As I drifted out of fantasies of backing a large horse over Tim Lindy's prone, helpless form and back to reality, Courtney—such an innocent-looking person!—commented to the girl on the other side of her: "I've got Dubois the Queer for second hour ...."

She'd done the unthinkable and said it in front of a teacher. Mrs. Sands either didn't hear or deliberately ignored her. I'd been so sure that if anyone on the entire face of the earth lacked the Weasel gene, this girl did. I couldn't make a sound for a few minutes, so any opportunity to speak out passed before I could grab it. Or, at least, I made that excuse to satisfy my conscience. Now more than ever, I knew this was a

88

day of opposites. I wouldn't be too terribly shocked if I *did* receive a written apology from Frank.

Right before I re-located my vocal chords, the brand-new Weasel said she'd never ridden before. "Well, then, you'd better have a gentle one," I quickly advised. "Ask the man to give you Misty."

The other time I'd gone riding with Mr. Balsam's classes was also the first time I'd ever ridden, period. So I'd asked for a gentle horse, and got Misty. Even though I enjoyed myself, I regretted not being more adventurous. Misty moved no faster than a slow walk, and she absolutely refused to cross mud. I had to dismount and lead her through it. A pretty horse, but not very cooperative. I wished the lousy Weasel much misery.

This time I decided I could handle a more spirited mount. I figured arrogant Tim Lindy would take a fast horse. I'd need one too if I hoped to be in a position to maim him if he took a fall.

I saw Tim climb out of Mr. Balsam's van when all the cars arrived at the stables. I must've glowered at him, because Mrs. Higuerra—who'd also driven a bunch of kids—came up to me and asked, "What's the matter, Sam?"

"Nothing, really. Just contemplating murder," I said, smiling at her.

Mrs. Higuerra knew me well enough not to call the police. "Well, Sam, just think about the penalty," she told me, walking away.

Think about the penalty, I repeated to myself. Didn't I always? So much that I had become totally paranoid from worrying what people might think of me.

I stopped dwelling on the subject and chose a sleek red roan named Jughead. He had spirit enough—more than enough. As we loped along the wooded trails, I kept him on the heels of Tim's horse, a dark gray. If we fell behind, I'd urge Jughead right back up. Call me a one-girl posse. In mid-pursuit, Jughead ran me into the trunk of a maple tree. Not all of me, just my left leg—but that much was bad enough. I knew I'd have a horrendous bruise, and I swore at Jughead, but I still pursued Tim. The pain lost its grip on my attention. In fact, I'd never had a better time without Bobby in my field of vision. Amazing I lived through so much fun—or at least amazing I managed to stay in the saddle. Jughead was *wild*.

We all rode into an open field, and everybody started galloping around—everybody except Jughead and me. He got it into his head right then and there he no longer wanted to move. My temper increased at seeing Courtney gallop by on Misty. "Thanks for recommending her!" she called to me. *Great. Wonderful.*

I'd always disapproved of kicking horses to motivate them. I'd thought of it as mistreatment, but with Jughead I changed my opinion. I kicked, and I yelled, but neither tactic budged him. Fortunately, we'd stopped right next to a bush, and I reached down to pull a stick from it.

I couldn't quite reach one.

"Here, I'll snag it for you," offered a voice. I looked back, turning in the saddle. I met the pale blue eyes of Timothy Lindy. He handed me the stick. I thanked him, swatted Jughead with a short, sharp *whuuup!* and rode away.

Tim must have thought me fairly bizarre. I stared at him like he'd suddenly broken out with green and purple spots on his homely face. None of this was supposed to be happening. Timothy Lindy was supposed to be mean and dirty-minded—not helpful to people stuck on wild horses. Even Maria's description hadn't prepared me for this. After all, she hadn't said anything *good* about him, had she?

Then the realization came. I had just *thanked* a Weasel! Not only had I said "thank you," but I had accepted his assistance. *Uggh! Yecch!* I put it all down to my shocked condition, and tried to turn Jughead back towards Tim. His help had not diminished my desire for vengeance. If anything, it increased it. I looked up at the clear sky, asking forgiveness for taking the stick from Timothy, and I noticed a mourning dove flying above me. I half-expected it to deliver a message from Frank. After this, nothing was impossible. I'm probably lucky it didn't drop anything else on me.

Jughead had a thing about open fields, I guess. He didn't like them. While I gazed stupidly up at the dove, he suddenly bolted for the woods. I could only hang on.

I pulled on the reins to turn him, but Jughead didn't care. I pulled with my full strength, but he didn't even seem to sense the hard steel bit in his mouth. We galloped past Mr. Balsam. I caught a glimpse of his droopily-mustached face as we passed. He looked like I probably looked when I took the stick from Tim Lindy. He sat there on his horse, watching me ride off into the sunset, or whatever I actually rode off into. I imagined him saying, like the end of a Lone Ranger movie: "Who *was* that masked girl?"

I could not get that horse to turn around. Fortunately, one of the stable employees came riding up the path. She caught Jughead by the bridle, slowed him down, turned him, and sent us back the way we'd come. I passed Mr. Balsam again and said, feeling silly, "Well, I'm back."

I never did run Tim over, and I'm still baffled by the whole day. I never had another one so completely different from everything I expected. When I described it for him, Mr. Dubois said it proved you can't put people into rigid categories. But even though it shot holes in my belief that Weasels were always completely despicable under every circumstance, I sort of enjoyed the day anyway. Especially the riding. I *liked* riding Jughead. Definitely not dull. I found out later, though, that the stable sold him because of his wildness—a pity. He was, all things considered, a pretty good Weasel-hunter.

I didn't enjoy what happened when I finally got back, though. My mom waited in the school parking lot to pick me up. As I got into the passenger seat of the old silver Pontiac, she greeted me with: "Guess what came in the mail today?"

"A letter for me from Frank Stallinger?"

"Who?" Mom looked puzzled for a moment. Then she said, "No. A letter for me and your father from the school board. There's a hearing on Mr. Dubois's continued employment, set for the evening of the last day of school. Sam, how long have you known he was in trouble without telling me?"

Chapter Nine

I played as innocent as kittenhood with my mother, so as not to implicate my father. Dad escaped, though Mom insisted she and I, at least, would attend Mr. Dubois's hearing. My father put his foot down and refused. Not that he didn't like Mr. Dubois—he barely knew him. If possible, Dad hated situations like the hearing even more than I did.

My own feelings on the subject were complex. I loved my mother for wanting to help defend Mr. Dubois, but I would have given up unlimited free concert tickets to any acts I could think of for the rest of my life if only: 1) Mom would change her mind and not go; 2) If she had to go, she wouldn't take me; or 3) If she had to go, and she had to take me, she'd just keep her mouth shut. I mean, Bobby still wasn't really speaking to me. I'd be lucky if he'd forget about my friendship with Mr. Dubois by even the *third* year of high school. If my mother made a spectacle of herself at this meeting....

But I didn't say any of this to my mother. I couldn't bear to have her—the woman who knew maybe even more than Denise did how much reason I had to care about Mr. Dubois—fully know my cowardice. I did, however, mention futility to her. Not the evening when she picked me up from horseback riding, but another time when the subject came up. I was helping her dry the dishes and put them away.

"It's just so useless anyway, Mom," I protested, gathering up the knives and forks I'd dried. I placed them in the correct drawer partitions, making as much rattling stainless steel noise as possible. "I bet you and Denise's parents are the only people on Mr. Dubois's side. The school board will listen to the majority, so you won't do any good."

"Even if that turns out to be the case," said my mother, pitching her voice above the clanging, "wouldn't you feel worse if we didn't go? If *only* Denise's parents gave him support? I want to do the right thing, even if it doesn't help Mr. Dubois keep his job."

Not long after this conversation, the last day of school finally arrived. At Turkey Creek, the last day of eighth grade is traditionally spent at a beach on Lake St. Clair. All the first hour classes are piled into buses and driven out there. No formal graduation, just (in theory, anyway) fun. Unfortunately, both Denise and Lisa were away helping the handicapped kids at some kind of camp. They had made a similar arrangement to mine with the kindergartners. They'd be back in time for Denise to come to the school board meeting with her parents. At any rate, I made plans to spend the day with Kim, the other girl who hung around with the three of us in Mr. Randolph's math class. Mr. Dubois told me he planned not to be there for beach day. Not only did he need to prepare for his hearing that night, but without the structure imposed by everyday classroom routine, he thought some kind of trouble might arise with him at its center. I understood. Not cowardice—I would've recognized that—but rather consideration for the very people who attempted to force him out of a job.

When that morning came, then, the sun shone brightly, a great day for the beach. I dressed, putting on a pair of knee socks with my shorts and pulling them all the way up. Not the best of fashion statements, but the big, ugly bruise I got when Jughead tried to scrape me off on the tree still glowed with lurid yellows and purples. I didn't want Bobby to see it, assuming he'd come anywhere near me.

I didn't want Bobby to see. As I pulled on a sneaker, it dawned on me the phrase probably explained every single stupid thing I'd done since January. At first I worried about Bobby discovering my friendship with Mr. Dubois. When it became obvious he had, I worried he'd never forget it. But did Bobby equal the entire answer? Every time I didn't stand up to a Weasel, I backed down because ... well, because I knew people—the popular people—would drag me through the raw sewage of middle school gossip. Could I hold my nose and bear that even if Bobby didn't exist? I didn't know.

Bobby *did* exist, though, and even if he didn't think me so awful for being friends with Mr. Dubois —after all, he *had* seen him kissing Ms. Evans on the lips—it wouldn't matter a bit. Even if Bobby really loved me, he could never take all the pressure he'd get from his popular friends if he went out with me. Not to mention his parents, at this point.

Maybe the whole problem was that Bobby's heart beat no more bravely than my own. I wondered, as I looked in the mirror to part my hair down the middle, what life would be like if Bobby acted more like

Denise. But maybe I loved him so much because he didn't. Aside from his beautiful brown eyes, of course. Maybe because deep down inside, the same mixture of fears ate at both him and me, I loved him. The only difference between us was Bobby had adapted, given in and become one of the popular ones, and I couldn't. I couldn't stand up to them, but I couldn't give into them completely, either. If I ever managed to rid myself of the fear, if I ever beat the whole popularity system, maybe I could help Bobby banish his fear, too. Maybe next year, at high school....

But my bravery next year as a student at Audubon High wouldn't do a damn thing for Mr. Dubois *now*, would it? I tried to shut out thoughts of having the means to help him if I really wanted to. I walked to school, deciding not to pick up Maria. She and I had not exactly stayed close since our disagreement over Tim Lindy.

Once there, I rode to the beach with my first hour class. Kim's first hour shared the bus with mine, so I shared a seat with her. Bobby sat far away from us, with some disgustingly attractive girl from Kim's class. Kim said she thought she saw Bobby glancing over at us a couple of times during the ride, but I trusted neither her vision nor her interpretation.

At the beach Kim and I started out a little bored. We'd decided a couple of days before we wouldn't get our hair wet and wind up looking like seaweed creatures from hell. So we didn't even bring our bathing suits. But we sat on a blanket, watching the water flow towards us and retreat again. We listened to our schoolmates shrieking and laughing as they paddled around dunking each other. We weakened rapidly. Finally I suggested we plunge in anyway— wet shorts and tank tops would only be a minor inconvenience. Bobby, after all, was hopeless until at least next fall. From the way he'd been ignoring me, he probably wouldn't even notice how hugely mutant my high forehead looked when I got my hair wet. Assuming he came anywhere near me.

Kim agreed. We took off our sneakers and socks and waded into the cool waters of Lake St. Clair, keeping a cautious eye out for dead fish. Kim still didn't wet her mousy blond hair, but I needed the comfort of complete immersion. First I turned over, lowering the back of my head into the water and letting the small waves lap over my ears. I closed my eyes against the sun and allowed myself to float for a while, so peaceful! Pure illusion, but I felt totally protected by the water, like nothing could ever hurt me—or anyone I loved.

Then I stood up, turned, took a breath, and dove under. Swimming underwater transformed me into something good, strong, and powerful. I loved the way the currents flowed past all the parts of my body. If, when older, I ever won the chance to make love with Bobby, I would want to do it in water. Sometimes I thought I might have been a dolphin in another life. Whenever I thought this, I wondered what I'd done to deserve my present ungraceful state.

I opened my eyes underwater. Murky, but not so murky as to cause me to run into submerged objects. Speaking of which, not much time passed before I saw some in my path—a pair of legs. The water was not clear enough for me to tell whether they belonged to a male or a female, but they ended in either boys' swimming trunks or girls' shorts. Not Kim's shorts— hers were white, these navy blue. I decided to surface before I got embarrassingly close. Besides, I was running out of air.

Since I didn't know who it would be, I turned around before surfacing. When I am wet, my back is my best side.

"Sam?"

I'd prepared for disaster, but still... not this. Not Bobby. I flipped my hair out of my eyes and quickly wiped my nose before I faced him. He, of course, was not wet above the waist and still appeared all my heart could desire. On the edge of my vision I saw Kim beyond him, looking about as stupefied as I'm sure I did. In an instant, however, she faded from my mind completely as I stared into those dark brown eyes, wishing to God my own green ones were not bloodshot, as I knew they had to be.

"Sam?" he repeated.

"Yes," I managed to answer. He'd hardly spoken to me since Mr. Dubois had come down with pneumonia, and now this! This, when I looked my absolute worst! I folded my arms across my chest, not in hostility, but because my sopping shirt clung to me and I didn't want him to know the extent of my flatness.

"Can I talk to you?" he continued, moving closer to me.

"Yes, yes, of course," I told him.

"In private," he said, gesturing to a grove of birch trees standing a small distance from shore. Together we waded back.

Then it dawned on me what was happening. This was it! The moment I'd been waiting for since I'd first met Bobby Bouchard. It didn't matter that I was sopping wet, that my forehead was too high, that my eyes were red. It didn't even matter that I associated with Mr. Dubois. Bobby loved me anyway, and he would finally ask me out, ask me to be his. The emptiness of all these weeks without speaking to me had turned his fear of unpopularity to boldness. Why else insist on privacy but to declare his love?

I walked with him toward the trees, and I couldn't control my shivering. He picked up my towel as we went past, shook the sand from it, and placed it gently around my shoulders. Needless to say, my shivering continued. I would remember the touch of his arm on my back forever, and soon... soon I would know the taste of those lips. I'd dreamed of this day so many, many times, though I'd never quite pictured it like this. I always thought I'd look better. But at least the setting provided as much romance as any I'd ever imagined. By the time we reached the shelter of the birches, the wind had risen a bit, and the silvery undersides of the leaves shivered almost as much as me.

Bobby led me to a grassy clearing in the midst of the birches, sat down, and motioned for me to join him. I sat down cross-legged, facing him, still staring into those magnificent brown eyes. Oh, God, what had I ever done to deserve this reward? I fought to keep the tears from coming, and the thought of Mr. Dubois and how I was failing him added to my unworthiness.

Bobby reached out and took my hand, still wet from the water, still trembling. "Sam," he said, "thank you for letting me talk to you. I know it must seem like I've been avoiding you, and I'm sorry if it upset you or hurt your feelings in any way."

"I-it's okay," I stammered.

"I just couldn't face you, I'm so ashamed."

Ashamed? Ashamed of what? His feelings for me? "You don't have to be ashamed," I whispered softly. I wished he would end this awkwardness and kiss me.

"But Sam! I know you know that I know better! Hell, I told you myself!"

"Told me what?" Granted, I did not have any experience with boys asking me out, but I was starting to think Bobby's technique a little strange.

"About seeing Mr. Dubois kiss Ms. Evans," said Bobby, urgently. "Sam, I know you're his friend. I don't know why, but if you like him, you must have a good reason. You're too smart to like anybody without a good reason. And ever since my mom told me about what happened at your house the night she was out 'informing' people about Mr. Dubois, I've hardly been able to look at you."

I could hear the waves coming to shore in the silence that passed between us then. And I began to realize Bobby was *not* about to profess his love. This was not *it*, the great *it* I had awaited so long. But what it *was* also held interest.

"I didn't know my folks had started with this stuff about Mr. Dubois until after it happened," Bobby continued. "By the time I realized, it would've looked weird if I'd told them what I'd seen, and they dropped out. If they even *would've* dropped out. If they *had* dropped out, though, Sam, everybody would have found out *why*. Everybody would've *known,* Sam, that I had come to Mr. Dubois's defense. Oh, Sam, I know I'm a coward, and I'm really sorry, but you know what it's like around here." His grip on my hand tightened, urging silently: *You know what it's like!*

Yes, I did. I knew exactly what it was like. But somehow I couldn't say it. I could only nod my understanding.

"But you, Sam! You could do it," Bobby said.

"What?" If he didn't think me an idiot by now, he never would.

"Save Mr. Dubois," he said. "You could say you saw him. And her. On the night of February 13th, at

100

the Sczechwan Palace. You could go to the meeting tonight and tell everybody."

The pain in my throat became unbearable. The tears overflowed my eyes, and the sobs began escaping. I knew for sure now Bobby hadn't called me to this secluded place to ask me out, but to confess he was just as messed up as I thought. As messed up as me. The dashing of my romantic hopes did not cause me to start crying, though a kind of connection existed. Like the way bad weather doesn't really *cause* you to have a cold, it just weakens you so when the virus *does* come along, you can't fight it off as well as normally. The virus in this case was that Bobby thought me brave enough to stand up and save Mr. Dubois, and I knew I wasn't.

"Sam, Sam! What's wrong?" Bobby asked, frantically moving to pat me on the back in what he thought would be a reassuring manner.

"I can't!" I wailed. "I'm just as scared as you are! Worse, maybe."

"You are?" A major revelation to him.

"Yes, and even if I wasn't, I still couldn't do what you say. Mr. Dubois made me promise not to."

"Huh?"

"When all this started," I said, "I told Mr. Dubois to tell the school board about his relationship with Ms. Evans. He said he wouldn't use her that way, and that the school board had no business knowing about his personal life. He said, 'What about the people who really are gay, or who really do have AIDS, who can't defend themselves by pointing out their straightness?'"

Oddly enough, Bobby understood my jumbled account. He gave a low whistle. "That's what Mr. Dubois said?" he asked.

"Yes."

101

"He must really be some guy, huh, Sam?"

"Yeah," I said.

"Too bad we can't do anything for him."

Yeah.

Bobby helped me up, and we stepped out of the birch grove. He left me with Kim, who, as soon as he'd passed out of earshot, demanded: "Well? Did he do it? Did he ask you to go out with him?" She'd obviously put things together the same stupid way I had at first.

"No," I told her, trying not to cry anymore. "But it was kind of nice, anyway."

Chapter Ten

Bobby rode home on the bus with the same girl he'd ridden with to the beach. I considered it a further sign that, while he cared about my feelings and—for some reason—even *admired* me as a person, he did not love me. Not only that, but, thinking back on our conversation in the birch grove, he must find my social status already so hopeless as to be totally expendable. Why else would he think *I* could give his restaurant evidence about Mr. Dubois and Ms. Evans when he could not?

Well, I forgave him. One, he was probably right. Two, he wasn't any worse a person than me. Maybe even a little better, because *he* had no particular reason to want to help Mr. Dubois. *Bobby* hadn't spent the better part of the last two years pouring out his troubles to the man.

So now I had to get through the meeting. From what I understood, Bobby'd probably be there, too. His parents—or his mom, anyway—had played a big part in "the movement" to rid Turkey Creek of Mr. Dubois. There might not be much I could do about Mr. Dubois's situation, but I could at least see to it Bobby saw a much better-looking me than at the beach this morning. Well, at least better in that my hair wouldn't be wet, my forehead would be covered, and my eyes wouldn't be red. Unless I started crying uncontrollably when Mr. Dubois lost his job. Everybody'd know where I stood then, wouldn't they?

Anyway, I couldn't *really* try to look *that* good for Bobby. My mother impressed upon me that we had to look like dignified, upstanding citizens so the school board would take our support for Mr. Dubois seriously. In other words, I had to dress like the very kind of strait-laced prude who most *wanted* to see Mr. Dubois lose his job. The irony of it struck me as I selected my most modest-looking cotton dress, and I fell back on my bed, laughing.

I readied myself slowly. Physically, I mean. Mentally, I knew I'd never be ready. My mother had already made herself the picture of responsible matronliness—quite a stretch from her usual style—and kept stopping in my bedroom doorway to glare at my lack of progress. At last, however, I could find no more finishing touches to make to my appearance. I let my mother drag me out to the car.

Mom kept up a steady stream of chatter about nearly everything in the known universe as she drove. Trying to help me feel less afraid, I guess, though she thought I only feared for Mr. Dubois. And I *did* fear for him, too. But honestly, I was more preoccupied with how all of this affected *me*. I managed to give Mom what I hoped were appropriate yes or no answers, even though I paid no attention to a word she said. I listened instead to the naggy little voice inside my own head. The one which kept saying, "You *can* do it, Sam. You *can* save Mr. Dubois if you *want* to." And I could do it without technically breaking any of the rules he himself had set for me. Revealing the charges against him to be completely made up did not quite equal using his relationship with Ms. Evans to prove them false. But to stand up, in front of all those popular kids who'd be there with their parents? To not only remove all doubt about my friendship for Mr. Dubois, but let him, Denise, and my mom know I could've stopped this all a long time ago? Right. A far greater chance existed they'd discover intelligent life on another planet by the end of the week.

My mother did not collide with any other cars, so we got there. Plenty of light remained in the sky. Because the school system was headquartered in our county seat, the school board used a room in the County Building for their meetings. The County Building stood on the shores of the Clinton River, near the river park. We had to walk on a sidewalk right next to the river to enter the building. I took a leaf from one of the oaks growing on the other side of the walk, and threw it into the river. I watched the current carry it swiftly away. The leaf, and the same water I looked at, would flow past Mr. Dubois's backyard later in the evening. This was another part of the same river we'd taken his sailboat through to get onto Lake St. Clair. I sighed.

The room for the meeting was already crowded when Mom and I arrived. Unusual, I knew, because Mrs. Higuerra had made us attend a regular school board meeting when we'd studied local forms of government. Tonight they'd even brought in extra chairs; the metal folding chairs on the outer perimeter looked considerably cheaper than the others.

I looked around. Oh yeah. A scene from one of my worst nightmares. Bobby sat there with his parents; and, as you might expect, so sat Billy Drake with the couple who'd inflicted him upon the world. But the rest of the kids attending with adults looked like a collection out of *Cheerleaders and Jocks Weekly*. The rulers of Turkey Creek Middle School social status had gathered *en masse*.

Mr. Dubois occupied a chair in the front row. Ms. Evans was at the meeting, but she was not seated next to him—he probably hadn't let her. Instead she sat in a group of other teachers who'd turned out in support of Mr. Dubois. Not all of the Turkey Creek staff had shown, but at least I counted a fair number of them.

Aside from the teachers, the only people I knew to be on Mr. Dubois's side were Denise, her little sixth-grade brother Paul, and her parents. They sat fairly close to the front as well, and unfortunately they saw us come in. They gestured at the two seats they'd saved for us. I tried to look invisible as I followed Mom up there. I scrunched down by Denise, and left the seat on the aisle for my mother. Hopefully, she'd shield me from most people's view.

A short bald man with glasses slinked up to the podium and apologized for the lack of air conditioning. The heat *was* pretty bad. "The janitor is trying to get it working; hopefully before this meeting is over, we'll have some relief."

"I used to go to school with him," my mother whispered. "He used to have hair."

"Since this is a special meeting called specifically to discuss one issue, I move we dispense with the usual preliminaries and get down to the business at hand," continued the bald man. He was seconded by one of his school board colleagues, an older woman with pointy cat glasses. He then proceeded to read the complaint against Mr. Dubois. He discussed Mr. Dubois's hospitalization with pneumonia, which he labeled "an illness which frequently accompanies

AIDS." He extended the formal request that Mr. Dubois submit to a blood test for HIV or provide the board with his hospital records. "How do you respond, Mr. Dubois?" Baldy asked, when he had concluded.

Mr. Dubois stood up and turned to face the majority of those seated. "I respond that my personal life is none of the Board's business, and I refuse to have an AIDS test." I wished for a moment Frank could be here to see Mr. Dubois's grace under pressure. Nothing in the man's reply sounded remotely effeminate. But then I realized how much Frank would've enjoyed watching Mr. D. lose his job, and I thanked God the Weasel was long gone.

In my thoughts, I'd predicted Baldy's next subject. "Having refused to be tested, Mr. Martin Dubois, will you resign your position as instructor at Turkey Creek Middle School?"

"No, I will not," said Mr. Dubois.

"Very well," said Baldy. "We will now open the floor to discussion as to whether or not you should be formally dismissed."

And that's what they did. Many statements came from many parents as to why Mr. Dubois should not be allowed to teach us. (Or, technically, teach other kids, since Denise and I would go to Audubon High next year.) These statements generally fell into two categories: well-intentioned, eloquent pleas not to expose their children to disease; and fearful cryings-out about not exposing their children to the obviously Godless homosexual. Drake's dad squatted with the latter camp. I couldn't help making a few small retching noises when he finished speaking, although I hoped people either didn't notice who'd done it or thought I'd had some natural kind of attack.

Amongst these various statements against Mr. Dubois struggled a few for him. Some of the teachers spoke up on his behalf. They, like Mrs. Marron—Denise's mom—talked about Mr. Dubois's civil rights and how badly the board was abusing them. But my mom stood up, and quietly but firmly talked of how much Mr. Dubois had helped her daughter. How he'd been the only one at Turkey Creek who'd noticed when her daughter had become severely depressed in the seventh grade. How her daughter's self-confidence had improved since he'd taken an interest in her. *Oh yeah.* I guess my self-confidence *had* improved, and I loved my mother for what she'd just done. But I slouched further down in my seat. The kids present didn't have to automatically assume Mom belonged to me if they didn't happen to see me sitting next to her. A strange quiet pervaded the room, though, for a few moments after my mother sat back down. Maybe she managed to move a few people.

But my mother's voice got swallowed up in a sea of negative others. Finally, when no more hands raised for permission to speak, Baldy announced: "The overwhelming majority of those gathered here, Mr. Dubois, favor your dismissal."

So it would really happen. I know I'd expected it, known it was coming. Now that we were right down to it, though, the pain of acceptance still surprised me. As a hard lump rose in my throat, Denise, on my other side, jumped up from her chair.

"No!" she shouted. "No! You can't do this! It's not right! It's all just a bunch of unfounded rumors — there's nothing wrong with Mr. Dubois!"

Every eye in the place turned to focus on Denise. Hopefully she'd understand when I tried to make *new* friends next year at Audubon. And yet, my heart screamed the same words as her mouth. I feared I'd be sick all over the pale beige tile floor.

"This is highly irregular, young lady," Baldy said to Denise. "How do you know the charges are unfounded? We are within our rights because he refuses to be tested. Despite the concerns of many parents here, his sexual preferences are not the real issue, but rather the suspicion he has a deadly communicable disease."

I had not told Denise Mr. Dubois had already been tested and turned up quite negative. I'd managed to honor his wishes in that, at least. So she had nothing really to tell Baldy, nothing that would do any good. But she murmured, "It's not *that* communicable," as she slid back into her folding chair.

Baldy heard her. He looked a bit uncomfortable, but he said: "We don't really know that. There are children who have AIDS for which no identifiable cause has been found. And what if Mr. Dubois has some kind of accident in class, something which involved blood..."

He trailed off, his words lost in a sudden deafening roar. The air conditioning had returned from the dead. Cool air started rushing past my face, definitely helping my fight against nausea. Cool air felt so good ... so good it reminded me of something. A time I'd felt really good ... and strong...

My dream! My *Lord of the Rings* dream, the one I'd had after Frank moved away. The one where the wind howled around me and I'd been wild and free and brave. The one where I sort of became the other Sam, the one in the books. I hadn't thought about those books in a long time. And alongside the memory of my dream, came the memory of the ending of the second book, *The Two Towers*. The memory of Sam

109

Gamgee throwing himself against the gates of Cirith Ungol after the orcs have carried Frodo inside. The despair because he is too late to get through the barrier, but the hope Frodo is not dead. The hope he can still save him, somehow, if he tries hard enough.

Suddenly, somehow, *I* am on my feet this time. As if out of some weird kind of background noise, I hear my mother's gasp, sounding far away, and my own voice, only a little closer, crying, "Wait!" When Baldy's eyes turn to me, scowling at yet another "irregularity," I manage to continue. "I know the charges are false."

Out of all the stares boring into me, I sense two in particular. Mr. Dubois looks at me through his glasses, his expression a strange mixture of gratitude and warning. He is touched I want to defend him, but he thinks I will tell all the things I know about him, all the things he didn't want to use in his own defense. I quickly shake my head in his direction. And then there is Bobby. He actually smiles at me. Even though he knows I cannot tell about Mr. Dubois and Ms. Evans, he has every confidence I have thought of *something*. No wonder he doesn't see me as an object of lust. He *respects* me too much!

"And how do you know?" Baldy asks me.

"Because it's all my fault," I say softly. But since the entire room had fallen still when I spoke up the first time, most of it managed to hear me over the air conditioner. My mother and Denise definitely heard, and looked appropriately shocked.

"What do you mean?" asked Baldy.

Now that I had begun, I prayed I'd be able to finish without passing out. On the other hand, I *could* pass out, and then later claim temporary insanity, or demonic possession. But no. I took a deep breath and tried to suppress my wooziness. "Well," I continued, trying to get more volume out of my shaky voice, "we've had the rumors Mr. Dubois was gay for a long time. But there were never any AIDS rumors—not serious ones—until Mr. Dubois went into the hospital.

"Before I knew he was out with pneumonia, I went down to his classroom in the morning to see him. I saw the substitute there about the same time Billy Drake came up to me. He told me Mr. Dubois was in the hospital. I asked him if he knew what was wrong with Mr. Dubois, and he said no. He also said, in a real snide tone, 'Gee, I wonder, don't you?'

"I'm sorry. This isn't a popular position, I know," I confessed to my peers in the audience, "but Mr. Dubois is my friend. He's helped me with all sorts of stuff, like my mom said. So everybody calling him names and insinuating things really got to me. When Drake used that tone, I just lost it. I yelled at him and said, really sarcastic, something like: 'Right. I just bet he's in the hospital because he's dying of AIDS.' And Drake goes, 'I bet you're right, Samantha,' like it hadn't occurred to him until then.

"By lunchtime that day," I concluded, "it was all over the school Mr. Dubois was in the hospital with AIDS. And my friend Denise told me Drake was the one who passed the rumor to her. I'm only sorry I waited so long to try and fix this."

I'd gestured to Denise as I sat back down, so Baldy turned to her and asked if the part concerning Drake was true. She nodded.

"Very well, then," said Baldy, returning his attention to me. "Is this William Drake present here tonight, Miss?"

Oh no. I knew where this was going. I had done it, I had thrown myself on the hari-kari sword of unpopularity, and IT WASN'T EVEN GOING TO WORK! Because everything now depended on a Weasel telling the truth. When Drake denied my accusations, it'd be all over. Nevertheless, I said "yes" to Baldy. What choice did I have?

"Will William Drake please identify himself to the Board?" Baldy requested.

Hell, he wouldn't even stand up. Well, maybe his parents would make him. Of course, they'd expect him to deny what I said; their pressure gave him all the more reason to lie. Sure enough, I saw his mother prod him to his feet. "I am William Drake," he managed, in a voice even shakier than mine had been.

"Is what this young lady told us true?" Baldy demanded.

A lengthy pause followed. I glared at Drake like my eyes were diamonds, cutting glass. But his folks stared at him expectantly, too. Drake, however, didn't look at me or his parents. When I pinpointed the object of his gaze, it proved none other than Denise. And if I'd been glaring at him, it was a benevolent glance compared to what she sent him with her eyes. What's harder than diamonds? Denise's stare, I guess. A small measure of relief—obviously she still held him more responsible than she did me.

In Denise's rage, however, Drake apparently found hope. His face lit up. "Yes," he declared. "Samantha is absolutely right."

I nearly fell out of my chair.

"You mean the charges are based on nothing more than this?" Baldy demanded.

"Yes," Drake repeated. "I started it all myself."

Baldy appeared a bit confused for a moment, then whispered amongst his colleagues. Finally, a consensus was reached. Meanwhile, across the aisle,

Drake's dad had dragged him back down into his seat by his shirt collar, presumably scolding him. The tension could be seen, but Mr. Drake held his voice too low for me to hear the words. Nothing, however, seemed to wipe the smile off Drake's face. After all, Denise had stopped glaring.

Baldy rapped his knuckles on the podium for attention. Eventually, he got it. "In light of this last testimony," he announced, "I would like to move the disciplinary measures against Mr. Martin Dubois be dropped and this meeting be adjourned." A middle-aged female board member with short hair who'd looked disgusted throughout the proceedings seconded the motion.

"May I see a show of hands?" asked Baldy. "In favor of the motion?"

Certainly, not all of the adults in the room raised their hands. Notable exceptions included the Drakes. But when Baldy asked for those against the motion to be counted, nobody responded.

We won. I couldn't believe it. We won. My life was probably ruined, but Mr. Dubois would keep his job. As people began filing out of the room, Mrs. Marron suggested we all celebrate by going out for ice cream.

"Let's ask Mr. Dubois and Ms. Evans to come with us," put in Denise, after Mom agreed. Apparently Denise had told her folks the two were a pair, and Mom remembered me mentioning Ms. Evans from the sailing trip, so they were not surprised. They sent me over to ask them.

Mr. Dubois hugged me when I got to him.

"You're not mad, then?" I asked.

"Well, I *was* looking forward to appealing, fighting this all the way to the Supreme Court, and maybe setting a precedent. But I guess I can find something else to do," chuckled Mr. Dubois. He exchanged a meaningful look with Ms. Evans.

"No," I said. "I mean for waiting so long to tell what I knew."

"No, Sam," he replied. "I know exactly what it took for you to do it at all. I'm just glad you did. Almost as much for you as I am for me."

I asked him and Ms. Evans about the ice cream. Just as they said they'd come along, I felt a hand on my shoulder. My body knew before my mind, and I shivered. I spun around to find Bobby. I didn't see his parents anywhere.

"I couldn't help overhearing, Sam," he said. "Can I come, too?"

"Sure," I told him. "What about your folks?"

"I told them I'd get a ride home with a friend. Really cool what you did, Sam."

"Thanks. I should've done it sooner."

"Well, at least you did it," said Bobby, looking a little embarrassed. I hoped it was because he could not have stood up like I had, and not because he began to regret possibly being seen with me.

As surprised as I was to have Bobby celebrating with us, I still remembered to search for Drake. I wanted to invite him, too. After all, I couldn't have done it without him. But apparently his folks had dragged him off already. Just as well. Denise may have stopped glaring at him, but she probably would have killed me if I'd encouraged him like that.

After tonight, I have no idea what next year at Audubon High will be like. But maybe it won't be too bad. Maybe kids are a little more mature there. In any case, I've promised Mr. Dubois I'll come back to visit every once in a while and give him reports.

www.ingramcontent.com/pod-product-compliance
Lightning Source LLC
Chambersburg PA
CBHW020505030426
42337CB00011B/243